November 3 2008.

To the bird I'd most like to have on the back – if you know what I mean.

All my love,

[illegible]

THE NEW MOTORCYCLE YEARBOOK

1

SUPERCUTS
Harley-Davidson

THE NEW MOTORCYCLE YEARBOOK

1

The Definitive Annual Guide to all New Motorcycles Worldwide

Simon de Burton

MERRELL
First Published 2005 by
Merrell Publishers Limited

Head office
81 Southwark Street
London SE1 0HX
Telephone +44 (0)20 7928 8880
Email mail@merrellpublishers.com

New York office
49 West 24th Street, 8th Floor
New York, NY 10010
Telephone +1 212 929 8344
Email info@merrellpublishersusa.com

www.merrellpublishers.com

Publisher Hugh Merrell
Editorial Director Julian Honer
US Director Joan Brookbank
Sales and Marketing Manager Kim Cope
Sales and Marketing Executive
Nora Kamprath
Managing Editor Anthea Snow
Editor Claire Chandler
Junior Editor Helen Miles
Art Director Nicola Bailey
Junior Designer Paul Shinn
Production Manager Michelle Draycott
Production Controller Sadie Butler

British Library Cataloguing-in-Publication Data:
De Burton, Simon
The new motorcycle yearbook 1 : the definitive annual guide to all new motorcycles worldwide
1.Motorcycles – Periodicals 2.Motorcycles – Design and construction – Periodicals
I.Title
629.2'275'05

ISBN 1 85894 280 2

Produced by Merrell Publishers Limited
Designed by Untitled
Copy-edited by Richard Dawes

Printed and bound in China

Page 2
Harley-Davidson V-Rod: the fastest-ever production Harley.
Pages 4–5
The MT-01: Yamaha's naked bruiser.
Pages 8–9
Dreamcraft Studios DCS-001: no more than six of these £150,000, hand-built cruisers are expected to be made.
Pages 268–69
The radical Confederate F113 Hellcat

CONTENTS

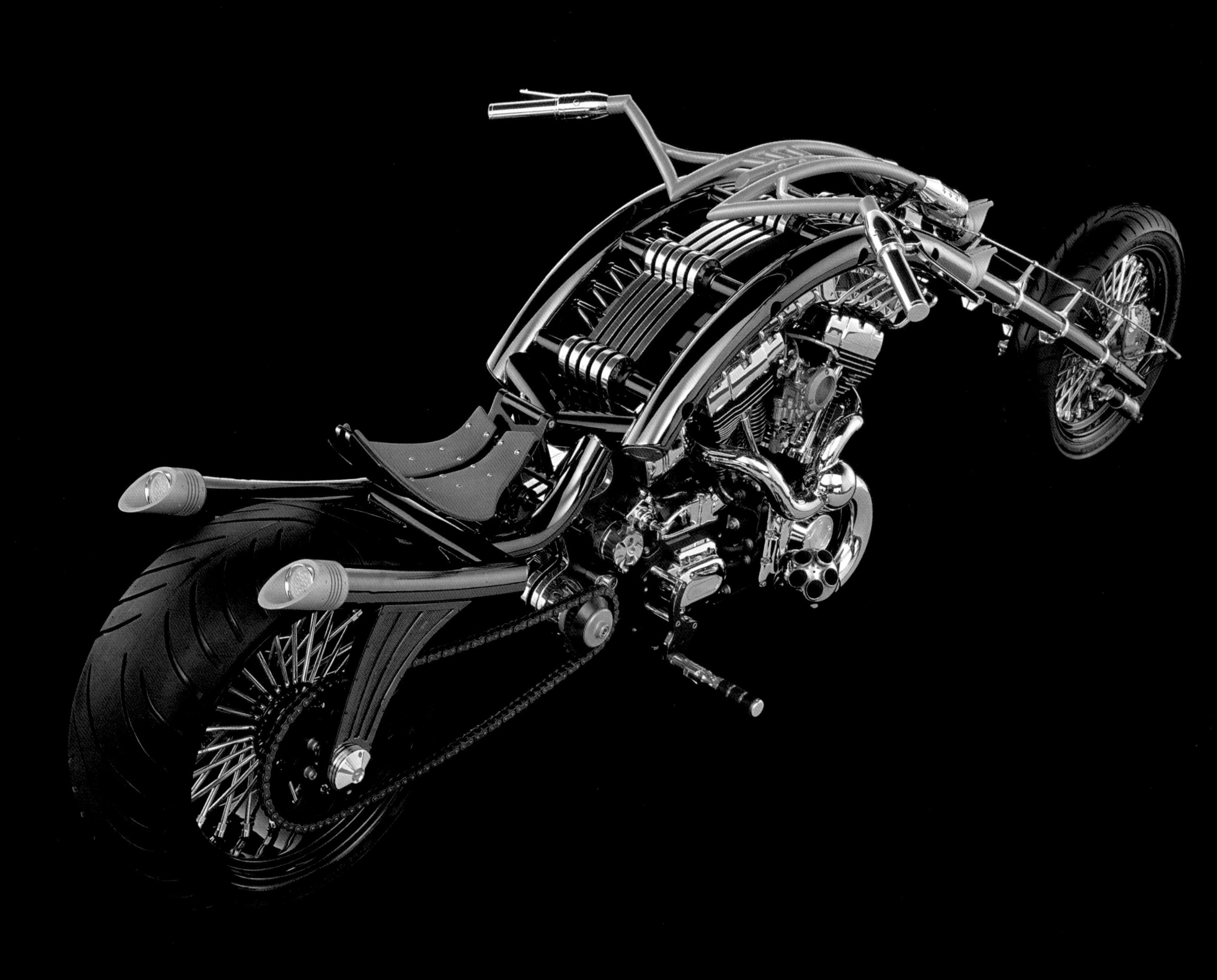

TRENDS, HIGHLIGHTS AND PREDICTIONS

Look back a little more than two decades and the world of motorcycle design appeared to be stagnating. Global sales of new machines were approaching the nadir of a decline that began during the 1970s and the market, such as it was, looked set to be dominated for ever by what had become known as the 'UJM'.

The acronym stands for 'Universal Japanese Motorcycle', a rather derogatory term that was coined by the old-school enthusiasts who blamed the likes of Honda, Suzuki, Kawasaki and Yamaha for homogenizing motorcycling with their essentially similar products.

What UJM referred to in particular was the medium-to-large-capacity, across-the-frame, four-cylinder models that had become the staple of every Japanese marque. Apart from oddities such as Yamaha's SR500 four-stroke single-cylinder machine (made in the mould of much-revered British 'thumpers' such as the BSA Gold Star), a selection of unremarkable trail bikes and the last remaining middleweight two-strokes, every other offering from the Land of the Rising Sun seemed to be a 'four-stroke four'.

Of the European marques, BMW continued to enjoy a reasonable success catering for the mature, hard-riding tourist with its horizontally opposed 'twins'; while Moto Guzzi drew a few diehard buyers with its agricultural, v-twin machines, best known for their unreliable electrical systems. The once glorious names of Ducati and MV Agusta barely registered on the sales graphs and as for Triumph, the revered British brand, that name was history and looked set to remain so.

But around 1985, despite the uncertainty of the market, a sea change began to occur in motorcycle design as Japanese manufacturers started to narrow the divide between the machines they built for the racetrack and those they built for the road. At the vanguard of motorcycling's new order was Suzuki, with its GSX-R750 Hyper Sports model.

Before this arrived in 1985, it seemed *de rigueur* for road bikes to have heavy steel frames, narrow wheels and tyres, and suspension that could easily be pushed beyond its limits. Big-bore Japanese motorcycles were famous for being good in a straight line but hopeless on the bends, which, if nothing else, provided an income for the after-market frame builders.

The GSX-R750, however, rewrote the rule book with its pure racetrack looks, powerful engine and ultra-light weight resulting from extensive use of aluminium alloy and magnesium. And its handling was way ahead of what had gone before.

Other manufacturers quickly followed suit, with Kawasaki introducing its GPZ600 R (another milestone machine, being the first to show that 'middleweight' engines could be more than 550 cc) and Honda bringing out its CBR 1000 and 600 models.

Once the template for these high-power, low-weight, maximum-performance machines had been established it seemed only to be a matter of refining the formula. Soon we were seeing dramatic new developments almost every year as the line between race technology and 'roadability' became ever more blurred.

Around 1985, despite the uncertainty of the market, a sea change began to occur in motorcycle design as Japanese manufacturers started to narrow the divide between the machines they built for the racetrack and those they built for the road.

Left
Kawasaki's state-of the-art ZX-6R.
Above
Honda's track-ready CBR 600RR.

Giant leaps in micro-electronics meant that features such as contactless ignition and fuel injection – once the exclusive domain of the more exotic motor cars – became common on motorcycles, making them more efficient, more reliable and easier to ride than ever before.

Then, as the 1980s gave way to a new decade, manufacturers became increasingly imaginative with their engine configurations. They continued to build smooth, quiet and reliable four-cylinder powerplants, but Italy's Ducati was showing strong signs of a revival with the growing success of its more earthy v-twin (or, strictly speaking, l-twin) racers and road bikes, so the Japanese began working on their own interpretation of the high-performance twin-cylinder machine.

A REVITALIZED INDUSTRY

Suddenly the world of motorcycle design was looking a lot more varied and lively and, coincidentally, people seemed to have both more spare money and more free time. There was a revival of interest in motorcycle racing, more people were taking up motorcycling as a leisure activity (both on and off road), and, as the world's cities and towns became ever more congested, the 'powered two-wheeler' showed itself to be one of the few viable options for anyone who wanted to get from A to B independently and as quickly as possible.

Ever-stricter emissions standards proved to be an unexpected benefit to riders of small-capacity bikes as manufacturers were forced to find ways of making clean four-stroke engines for scooters and lightweights that performed in a similar way to the old two-strokes. This advance meant cleaner, quieter, smoother small bikes, and sales of models such as Vespa's 'twist-and-go' ET4 sky-rocketed. These entry-level machines got more people on to two wheels and, inevitably, a percentage of them 'got the bug' and decided to progress up the ladder of engine capacity.

A good proportion of the growing disposable income was being spent on sports bikes, which, by the mid-1990s (following the introduction of Honda's phenomenal Fireblade in 1992) had entered a whole new realm. The superbikes of old – heavy, un-faired, ill-handling beasts rarely capable of more than 190 km/h (120 mph) – had been replaced by race-inspired rockets that offered easy 275-km/h (170 mph) performance, blinding acceleration, pin-sharp braking and on-rails handling for the price of a basic family hatchback.

Among the buyers were the so-called 'born-again bikers' in the forty-five-plus age bracket, who suddenly found themselves with the cash to spend on a big new motorcycle twenty or more years after they thought they had given up two wheels for good.

What these returnees had missed, however, was how the evolution of machines such as the old Honda 750s and Kawasaki 1000s they remembered from the 1980s had been dramatically fast-forwarded.

Suddenly a 600-cc motorcycle could be wheelied off the throttle and stopped dead. They also went round corners smartly and could out-accelerate even the most exotic supercar.

Above
The Triumph Rocket III with the largest capacity engine ever fitted to a production motorcycle: 2.3 litres.

The downside is that such machines are invariably too demanding for the ability of the average owner, which has resulted, at best, in lots of lost driving licences and, at worst, in the types of accident that give the anti-motorcycling lobby valuable ammunition.

So where does all this leave the state of motorcycles and motorcycling today, and what about the future? Over the past couple of years sales have failed to maintain their strong momentum but manufacturers continue to produce ever-better products.

The flagships of any marque's range remain the 'super-sports' models, as these define the perceived abilities of a brand – year after year, Japan's 'Big Four' compete with one another to refine and improve the ballistic missiles that they call 'sports bikes'.

And each year it seems impossible that their products could ever do what they are designed to do any better; yet each year a fraction of a second is shaved off a 0–100 km/h (0–60 mph) time, a tiny increment is added to a top speed, and a few valuable grams are trimmed from component parts.

SPEED IS NO LONGER KING

At last, however, it is starting to look as though the major manufacturers have finally conceded that enough is enough when it comes to outright speed and are now concentrating instead on refining frames and handling ever further. Honda is currently obsessed with keeping all the weight of its sports bikes low down and in the centre of the machine, while Kawasaki is offering racetrack technology with 'radial' brake calipers and 'slipper' clutches.

And make no mistake: buyers want road-going machines to look and behave as much as possible like the racers piloted by their track heroes – in fact, it is one of the most important factors in influencing sales.

But modern motorcycles are not just about the fastest race-replica rockets, for it seems that many riders have become a little weary of the downsides of such machines. A commonly cited drawback is that they are invariably far from comfortable, thanks to their competition-inspired, low-crouch riding positions.

Out on the open, winding roads where these bikes belong, such a seating position works well, allowing the rider to move easily from one side of the machine to another as it is made to flow rapidly from bend to bend; but in the urban jungle a racing crouch is literally a pain.

Some riders, too, have come perilously close to losing their licences on bikes such as these, through a combination of an excess of both performance and speed traps. Others complain about spiralling insurance premiums (sports bikes are particularly prone to theft as they can be broken down into parts that are easy to sell on), while, for many, the cost of maintaining a machine that is so powerful that it eats through an expensive rear tyre every 5000 km (3000 miles) simply becomes untenable.

It is because of people like this that, as *The New Motorcycle Yearbook* demonstrates, the relatively young 'supermoto' category is booming. These

predominantly single-cylinder, four-stroke machines offer the potential for grin-inducing fun thanks to their excellent power-to-weight ratio, yet they make highly practical commuter machines too.

They are cheap to buy and cheap to maintain, yet, with their aggressive looks and sound, fat tyres and general 'attitude', they pack as much street cred as the sleekest sports bikes. In fact, the supermoto class has grown to such an extent that manufacturers such as KTM have now taken it a step further by producing models with powerful, 1000-cc, twin-cylinder engines. These maintain the essential supermoto characteristics but make for a motorcycle that is even more versatile as it has better long-distance capability than a 500-cc or 600-cc single-cylinder machine.

There seems little doubt that, now that KTM has set the ball rolling, all the other major manufacturers will follow its lead and produce their own versions of the 'super supermoto'. But what is really interesting is that it has taken a relatively small firm to make the first move in that direction.

This is because the twenty-first century is proving to be the era of the niche manufacturer. KTM has grown from a name once known only to a hard-core of off-road racing enthusiasts to one of the most admired brands in the industry. The same is true of Ducati, which has capitalized on its sporting heritage and recent racing success (and maximized its marketing potential) to become the 'cool' motorcycle brand for affluent thirty-somethings the world over.

And let's not forget Triumph, the great British brand bought back from the dead by businessman John Bloor in 1991 and now well and truly a player on the world motorcycle scene. Not only is the Leicestershire company making a profit, it is making all the other brands sit up and take notice.

'REAL MOTORCYCLES'

Triumph's extraordinary Rocket III, the largest-engined production motorcycle ever made, now has a long waiting list and its new sports tourer, the Sprint ST, is being hailed as one of the finest machines in its class. Then there's the ultra-aggressive Speed Triple, which had buyers' mouths watering the moment it was unveiled in late 2004, and the promise of great things to come on the sports-bike front with the 680-cc triple due in 2006.

Triumph has also become well established in the 'retro' market, where it appealed to many people's sentiments with the launch of its modern-day Bonneville in 2000. At the time, the firm had this market more or less to itself, but now Ducati is getting in on the act with its Sport Classic range, Royal Enfield is increasing its model line and small-volume makers such as the American-based Norton Motorcycles are offering competition.

These are all essentially bikes aimed at the two-wheel enthusiast who likes so-called 'real motorcycles' where the engine can be seen, wheels have spokes and there is chrome to polish. But of late another important category of rider has emerged: the adventurer.

Above
The famous British name of Norton has been revived – by an American owner.

You will find more than a dozen new or updated 'adventure sports' machines in the pages of *The New Motorcycle Yearbook*, because this is an area that manufacturers all over the world are embracing wholeheartedly. As the planet becomes a smaller place through low-cost air travel and the number of true 'adventures' seems to dwindle, a trek into the unknown on a motorcycle remains one of the few ways of feeling you have really travelled.

Organized overland trips have grown hugely in popularity, as have the numbers of individuals or small groups going off on their own into the unknown, placing all their faith in motorcycles.

In 2004 actors Ewan McGregor and Charley Boorman made news around the world with their 'Long Way Round' tour on BMW Adventure machines, which took them from London to New York via Mongolia.

The BMW Adventure will undoubtedly remain one of the most popular motorcycles for epic journeys, but it faces stiff competition from manufacturers such as Honda, KTM, Aprilia and Triumph in an area of the motorcycle market that is increasingly important.

At the opposite end of the spectrum, motorcycle manufacturers appear to be making a major assault on the hitherto-untapped youth market. This new market is evidenced by the creation of machines such as the Sachs MadAss and the Yamaha Tricker, both of which take their inspiration from icons of street culture such as skateboards and BMXs. These new-generation bikes are hip-looking, lightweight, minimalist machines that are designed for pulling attention-grabbing stunts as much as for getting from A to B.

Yet getting from A to B is not, of course, to be overlooked. That is why manufacturers such as Honda and Malaguti are spending huge amounts of resources on refining and improving their commuter scooters with cutting-edge technology such as digitally encoded security systems that enable the use of keyless ignition, dual-mode gearboxes and even, as on Honda's Forza-Z, waterproof, vibration-resistant hi-fi systems.

Could anyone who rode a scooter in the 1970s ever have believed that such refinements would one day exist? Probably not. But one thing is for certain: there are even more futuristic developments in the offing.

Left
A BMW R1150 GS Adventure doing what it does best.
Above
Suzuki's Burgman is typical of the latest generation of luxury maxi scooters; this electronic 'key' will activate the Honda Forza's systems from a distance of several metres.
Opposite
Yamaha's Tricker is the coolest machine on the street if you're a 'youth'.

tricker pro

ADVANCES IN ENGINEERING

Four decades ago Honda unveiled a racing motorcycle that wowed the world. It was a 250-cc, double-overhead-camshaft machine like nothing seen before – because it boasted a six-cylinder engine that revved to 18,000 rpm.

Despite its diminutive capacity, the RC 166 was capable of an astonishing 241 km/h (150 mph) and a later variation, the RC 174, won seven out of eight world championship races in the hands of the British rider Mike Hailwood.

Yet the buying public had to wait more than a decade before the first six-cylinder Honda road bike went on sale, and when it arrived it bore little in common with the screaming RC models. The CBX, as it was called, was a hefty, 1000-cc machine that weighed in at 259 kg (570 lb) with a tank full of fuel, so, despite its 'super sport' tag, this was never going to be a machine for throwing around a twisty race circuit.

Contrast that with the Ducati 999 on which James Toseland won the 2004 World Superbike Championship and it soon becomes clear that track technology now reaches the road in months rather than decades.

While the 999s you find in the showroom have refinements such as lighting sets, indicators and speedometers, they are instantly recognizable as being related to the machines ridden by Toseland. Look more closely, of course, and you will discover that the engines of the race bikes are tuned to the nth degree – to a point that would be impractical for road use – and that no expense has been spared in the all-important art of weight saving.

Yet anyone with the inclination to do so could relatively easily transform their road-going Ducati 999, Honda Fireblade, Yamaha R1 or Suzuki GSXR-1000 into a competitive racer without having to resort to a major re-engineering programme.

This is because Ducati, Honda, Suzuki, Yamaha and all the other big manufacturers who value the profile afforded them by top-level competition have spent years bringing race technology to the road to the point where a standard production bike costing less then £10,000 is now the equal of the exotic factory racers of just a few years ago that cost hundreds of thousands to produce.

This can partly be explained by the fact that components are now cheaper and easier to produce than ever before, thanks to Computer Aided Design (CAD) and to Computer Aided Manufacture (CAM), which enables parts to be made to minutely close tolerances and finished to a far higher standard than in the past.

In addition, manufacturers have become extremely clever in the use of lightweight materials, employing alloys to make ultra-rigid frames that weigh just a few kilograms, carving engine internals from titanium, and replacing, wherever possible, metal with featherlight-but-strong carbon fibre.

Look up the latest Honda CBR 600RR, for example, in *The New Motorcycle Yearbook* and you will read that the Japanese firm is proud to boast that it has saved 64 grams (2.3 oz) on the weight of last year's bike by modifying the fuel-injection nozzles; add this to the 1.5 kg (3.3 lb) saved by paring down the frame and the

Big manufacturers who value the profile afforded them by top-level competition have spent years bringing race technology to the road to the point where a standard production bike ... is now the equal of the exotic factory racers of just a few years ago.

Left
It may have lights and turn signals, but the Kawasaki ZX-6R is just as happy on the track as on the road.
Above
The same applies to the Suzuki GSXR 1000 and Ducati's 999.

figures start to explain why the new machine is a full 6 kg (13.2 lb) lighter than its predecessor – more than enough to make a vital difference on the race track.

An additional benefit of bringing these mildly tamed race bikes to the road is that, in general, they are superbly reliable because the engines, brakes, frames and suspension units are directly related to the competition parts, which are engineered to withstand far higher stresses than most road bikes are likely to encounter.

INFLUENCE OF RACE TECHNOLOGY

In truth, the modern-day superbike not only has engine performance way beyond what can legally be exploited on public roads, it also has ancillaries that are firmly rooted in competition.

Kawasaki's new ZX-6R, for example, comes with a 'slipper' clutch as standard. Until very recently this was a feature that was only ever found on pure race bikes; in order to prevent rear wheel lock-ups, it is designed to 'slip' during the type of violent down changes necessary in racing. While this might sound excessive for road use, it is actually a useful safety feature that could prevent a spill on a slippery surface during a clumsy downshift.

The other hot new feature in 2005 is the radial brake. Rather than being bolted to the motorcycle's front forks from the side, radial brake calipers are bolted on to the forks from the rear. This may not sound important, but the theory behind the innovation is that bolts running from side to side cause an uneven braking action that is eliminated with the radial system.

Combine this with a radially mounted master cylinder with direct actuation from the handlebar lever and feedback is greatly improved, making it easier to brake hard without locking the wheel.

But perhaps the most significant benefit of race technology currently being put to use on road bikes is the use of mass centralization – the art of keeping as much weight as possible in the middle of the machine and as low to the ground as possible.

Honda's five-cylinder RC 211V was the first significant race bike to put this theory into practice, in 2002, although it has always been intrinsic to the design of Eric Buell's road bikes, which carry the exhaust system directly below the engine and the fuel as low down as possible.

Again, Honda's CBR 600RR is 2005's most cutting-edge road machine in this respect. Its rear suspension has been completely redesigned to allow the lower portion of the fuel tank to be set low down and far back in order that handling is minimally affected by all that sloshing liquid.

Yet as fast and fine handling as these machines are, the manufacturers assure us that there is a great deal more to come, and perhaps the most eagerly awaited machine of 2006 will be the Ducati Desmosedici RR.

Set to cost around £35,000, this will be a genuine, road-going race replica based on the fabulously powerful v-four track bike. That produces an estimated 172 kW (230 bhp) at the rear wheel, which seems an absurd amount for a machine ostensibly for road use,

yet buyers are queuing up to own one of the limited production machines, which will be hand-built by Ducati's race division at the rate of one per day.

Honda, too, is tipped to build a touring bike that uses a version of the RC 211V racer's v-five engine, while fans of Valentino Rossi's Yamaha M1 race bike – which uses a back-spinning crankshaft to reduce the gyroscopic effect caused by the wheels – hope to see such technology on the next-generation R1 sports machine.

A much newer manufacturer, meanwhile – the fledgling Czech firm of Blata – has already entered the GP fray with a 990-cc, V6-engined race bike that the firm claims produces 164 kW (220 bhp). Until now Blata has made only knee-high, 39-cc minimoto bikes, but it has gone in at the deep end with the high-revving V6, which it intends to develop into a road bike by 2006.

THREE-CYLINDER POTENTIAL

Yet it is the three-cylinder engine configuration that many manufacturers seem most interested in exploring for use in middleweight machines. Triumph has been leading the way with its 675-cc Daytona triple, MV Agusta is said to be contemplating a 650-cc three as an affordable entry into MV ownership and Yamaha has already developed a state-of-the-art three-cylinder powerplant for its top-of-the-range snowmobile – but it is feasible that it could be used in a motorcycle.

Perhaps surprisingly, the relatively small Italian manufacturer Benelli has been the first to bring the switchable electronic engine mapping found on race bikes to the road by incorporating the technology into its new TNT. Traction control systems are also on the way, and even the exciting-sounding 'launch control', which will use electronics to control wheel spin and wheelies caused by excessively sudden throttle opening and clutch engagement.

But it is not a Japanese or Italian superbike maker that is causing the greatest interest in the race world at the moment. It is a little-known American company named Motoczysz, run by millionaire motorcycle fan, Michael Czysz.

His C1 machine – with which he intends to enter the Moto GP – uses a radical chassis made entirely from carbon fibre, a v-four engine with contra-rotating crankshafts and twin clutches, front and rear radiators and a modern interpretation of the front forks with single shock absorber used by Ducati some twenty years ago.

Another American firm, meanwhile, has just completed thirty-one examples of a road machine that makes most race bikes look positively tame. The Confederate Wraith is powered by a 1650-cc v-twin that is said to be the most powerful engine ever used in a production American motorcycle.

The Wraith has a rigid-fork front end linked to a large, car-type pivoting wishbone to provide suspension through a shock absorber concealed within the steering head. The rider stretches out over a massive, tubular back-bone frame and sits on a saddle-type seat that contains lights and indicators.

However, it is not just road-going racers that benefit

Left
The radical Confederate Wraith.
Above
The Wraith's minimalist front end contrasts strongly with the retro appeal of a modern Triumph twin.

Above
Old-fashioned engineering has not hampered Harley-Davidson's success.

from this wealth of modern technology – street and 'naked' motorbikes do too, as well as cruisers, supermotos and, strange though it seems, retros.

The really great thing about the latest retro bikes is that they provide all the looks and the character of old-fashioned motorcycling with the benefits of modern engineering – and that usually means engines that start on the button (rather than after several hefty kicks) and no oil leaks.

Modern-day retros also produce the sort of power that engine tuners forty years ago would have given their eye teeth to achieve; and deliver it in a smooth, manageable way that makes machines such as Triumph's Bonneville a delight to ride in any conditions – which could not always be said of the original 1960s versions.

For, although we look at the products of old through rose-tinted spectacles, the truth is that they were often the machines that gave motorcycling a reputation for being dangerous. There is no doubt that it will be much easier to get out of trouble on a 2005 Ducati Sport Classic – which has pin-sharp brakes, taut suspension and sticky tyres – than it would have been to avoid a collision on the 1970s bikes (with their narrow tyres, drum brakes and bouncy, unprogressive suspension) whose looks they emulate.

Even so, many motorcyclists appreciate a certain 'rawness' in the machines they ride. How else could Harley-Davidson, for example, have become and remained so successful? The average Harley rider loves the throbbing vibration of the marque's unrefined v-twin engines and many fit extra-loud exhausts so that great American sound – which was once subject to a patent application – can be enjoyed all the more easily.

That may soon have to come to an end in Europe, though, as stringent EU noise regulations due to be introduced in 2006 will require all new road bikes to pass a strict ride-by noise test that will measure not only the exhaust decibels but also the sound made by everything from the air intake to the tyres, engine and drive train.

It seems that the bureaucrats may be taking the example of one of the first production Harley-Davidsons a little too seriously – built in 1906, it was called the Silent Gray Fellow.

THE MOTORCYCLES

HONDA

TOURERS

BMW R1200 RT

Engine
1200 cc, air-cooled, single-overhead-camshaft, twin, four-valve, four-stroke
Power
82 kW (110 bhp) @ 7250 rpm
Torque
108 Nm (80 ft lb) @ 5500 rpm
Gearbox
Six-speed with overdrive
Final drive
Shaft
Weight
259 kg (571 lb)
Top speed
209 km/h (130 mph)

Ask any experienced long-distance rider what is the best new, no-frills touring motorcycle on the market and there is a good chance they will recommend BMW's all-new R1200 RT.

If you are looking for lots of chrome, cruising lights and street cred, the flat-twin BM is not for you. But if you are looking for a highly efficient tool capable of racking up incredible distances, it's practically impossible to beat.

Despite the apparently outmoded air-cooled, twin-cylinder engine, the R1200 RT is capable of cruising all day at three-figure speeds (partly owing to its new six-speed gearbox), yet its fuel economy is unrivalled in its class. Ridden gently, this bike can achieve 21.2 kmpl (60mpg) with ease. Combine this with a fuel capacity of 27.3 litres (6 gallons) and the result is the best range of any production tourer.

A large amount of torque produced at low revs means the engine hardly breaks sweat at motorway speeds and this, along with huge engine braking and the very effective angular-fronted fairing, height-adjustable screen and 'wind spoiler' mirrors, makes the R1200 RT one of the least tiring motorcycles ever built.

The standard luggage set-up provided with the bike (an integrated rack and two BMW System cases) will hold enough kit for a long weekend for two, but this can be augmented from BMW's accessory range. The two-piece seat offers three-position height adjustment, and other practical touches include electrically adjustable suspension for solo, pillion or luggage use, twin electric sockets for powering items such as an intercom or heated clothing, a jump-start connection and a weather-insulated stereo system. The options list even includes a pop-out, fairing-mounted cup holder.

BMW's specially developed Telelever front suspension and Paralever rear suspension make for surprising handling for a touring bike, while the brakes – linked and operated by an electro-hydraulic system with ABS – require only two-finger pressure to stop the machine very smartly indeed.

Although this is an undeniably large bike, the low centre of gravity that results from the flat-twin engine layout makes the R1200 RT both surprisingly light to handle and unexpectedly easy to lift on to its centre stand.

Its predecessor, the R1150 RT, was BMW's most successful touring bike ever, and this is a mantle the R1200 RT seems certain to assume.

BMW

BMW

BMW

BMW K1200 LT

BMW motorcycles have long been the choice of touring riders who want to put in some good distances. The marque earned its reputation for long-range bikes through a combination of build quality, reliability and the simplicity of the classic BMW 'boxer' engine.

In 1999, however, the German firm wowed the motorcycle world with the original K1200 LT, a radical and refined 'über tourer' of such huge dimensions that, at first sight, it appeared almost unrideable. But rideable it was – and how. Despite its 380-kg (838 lb) weight and unusual, swept-back handlebars, the LT proved itself a sweet handler that could be banked over until its thick rubber fairing protectors threatened to touch tarmac.

The model remains the flagship of the BMW motorcycle range, although the latest version boasts numerous updates over the original. Add all the extras to the premium-line LT Lux, for example, and you'll ride away on a bike that boasts fully integrated panniers and top box, two auxiliary power sockets, an electrically adjustable screen, a map light, front and rear mudguards and a unique push-button, electrohydraulic centre stand.

And there's much more: a four-speaker CD/radio with CD multichanger, hazard warning lights, 'soft touch', independently heated seats, heated grips, cruise control, high-level brake light, top box luggage rack and BMW's own Motorrad Navigator II satellite navigation system.

An on-board LCD computer display gives information on everything from fuel level to ambient temperature, and also available are central locking, chrome passenger footplates and even ground-level lighting.

In common with most super tourers, such a comprehensive specification inevitably leads to excess weight and earlier LTs were criticized for lacking the engine power needed to pull the whole lot along. BMW has responded by squeezing an additional 12 kW (16 bhp) from the engine and altering the electronic fuel mapping to ensure a more free-revving, sporty feel and an impressive power surge that lasts from 5000 rpm to the red line at 8000 rpm.

But perhaps the most extraordinary feature of the new LT is its all-enveloping fairing, which allows it to be ridden in the type of conditions that motorcyclists usually baulk at. Such is its efficiency that, in all but the most torrential rain, a rider of average height should remain completely dry as long as the bike is moving.

Engine
1171 cc, liquid-cooled, fuel-injected, four-cylinder, four-stroke
Power
87 kW (116 bhp) @ 7000 rpm
Torque
120 Nm (88 ft lb) @ 5250 rpm
Gearbox
Six-speed
Final drive
Shaft
Weight
387 kg (853 lb)
Top speed
209 km/h (130 mph)

HARLEY-DAVIDSON FLHTCSE SCREAMIN' EAGLE

Engine
1690 cc, air-cooled, twin-camshaft, v-twin, two-valve (push-rod-operated)
Power
56 kW (75 bhp) (est.) @ 5000 rpm
Torque
117 Nm (86 ft lb) @ 4250 rpm
Gearbox
Five-speed
Final drive
Belt
Weight
377 kg (831 lb)
Top speed
185 km/h (115 mph)

Their critics call them dinosaurs, but why should Harley-Davidson go down the road of homogenized, plastic-clad, whisper-quiet motorcycles when the brand name is among the five most recognized in the world?

This latest version of the legendary Electra Glide unashamedly boasts the DNA of the original, which appeared in 1965, getting the first part of its name from the addition of an electric starter, and that's just the way Harley fans want it to be. They want their Electra Glide to look like an Electra Glide, and the firm knows this, so it is no surprise that the Screamin' Eagle special is more cosmetic makeover than engineering redesign.

The list of extras on this limited model, produced by the marque's Custom Vehicle Operations (CVO) unit, runs to almost seventy individual items. To the uninitiated, features such as a cloisonné-enamel badge on the new, clear-glass headlight and chrome trim on the saddlebags (not panniers, please) are hardly anything to write home about, but to a Harley fan they are details that set this Electra Glide apart from all the others.

The Electra Glide remains the true incarnation of the American freedom machine. Its 1690-cc, v-twin engine is harsh and raucous by Japanese standards, but that helps make it a Harley; the fairing isn't a streamlined, wind-tunnel-developed, all-protecting shield – it's an Electra Glide fairing; the handling of the machine is slow and heavy – just like an Electra Glide should be.

If you want a long-distance tourer, there are plenty of cheaper, better-built, more reliable and smoother-running motorcycles to choose from, but, as any Harley fan will tell you, every one of the companies that make them can but dream of capturing Harley-Davidson's share of the market.

In the right context – a sun-drenched day on Route 66, say – an Electra Glide is impossible to beat as a fulfiller of dreams and fantasies. And, so long as you're happy to take it easy, you cruise along in relative comfort thanks to the rubber-mounted engine, luxurious saddle and fairing-mounted CD player – which doesn't, incidentally, play only *Born to Be Wild*.

HONDA

HONDA
HONDA

HONDA GL 1800 GOLD WING

When Honda launched the Gold Wing back in 1975, who could have predicted that the model would remain in production long enough to warrant a thirtieth-anniversary edition? Or that it would look like this?

Such is the loyalty and following inspired by the 'Wing' that the model has almost become a brand within a brand. There are Gold Wing owners' clubs throughout the world and, for motorcyclists who want the nearest thing there is to a two-wheeled, roofless car, this is the only bike to have.

While the original Gold Wing was considered a tourer merely because it had a 1000-cc, liquid-cooled engine and shaft drive, the latest incarnation boasts a specification that makes its ancestor seem positively pared down.

Over the years the traditional flat-four engine has sprouted an extra couple of cylinders, making the latest Gold Wing powerplant probably the smoothest and most refined motorcycle engine ever created. Liquid cooling all but eliminates mechanical noise, ensuring the machine produces only a whisper-quiet hum that belies its cylinder capacity of more than 1800 cc.

Refinements abound, from the four-light, wrap-around fairing with wind-tunnel-designed airflow ducts and electrically adjustable screen to the rear-mounted, built-in boot locker with side-mounted FM aerial. The bike also offers an RDS entertainment system, cruise control, computer controlled, push-button suspension adjustment, a throne-like, electrically heated seat with additional stereo speakers and storage pockets and a pair of copious, colour-matched panniers.

With a 30-litre (6.6 gallons) fuel capacity, the latest Gold Wing is capable of travelling more than 400 km (250 miles) between fill-ups. Yet it is designed to remain comfortable for far greater distances and it is not uncommon for fanatics of the model to ride more than 1000 km (620 miles) in a single day.

There is, of course, a price to pay for all this luxury, and in the case of the Gold Wing it is a vast weight penalty: without rider, passenger or a change of clothes on board, this machine tips the scales at 363 kg (800 lb). As a result it needs a car-type linked braking system to slow it down and an electrically controlled reverse gear to assist parking.

All in all an undeniably excessive motorcycle, but this, it seems, is part of the Gold Wing's legendary appeal.

Engine
1832 cc, liquid-cooled, fuel-injected, flat-six, four-stroke
Power
87 kW (116 bhp) @ 5500 rpm
Torque
167 Nm (123 ft lb) @ 4000 rpm
Gearbox
Five-speed with electric reverse
Final drive
Shaft
Weight
363 kg (800 lb)
Top speed
225 km/h (140 mph)

HONDA ST 1300 PAN EUROPEAN ABS

Engine
1261 cc, liquid-cooled, fuel-injected, v-four, four-stroke
Power
93 kW (125 bhp) @ 8000 rpm
Torque
117 Nm (86 ft lb) @ 6500 rpm
Gearbox
Five-speed
Final drive
Shaft
Weight
283 kg (624 lb)
Top speed
233 km/h (145 mph)

For those who are seeking Honda reliability in a large-capacity touring bike yet don't want to join the Gold Wing clan, the answer is to buy a Pan European.

Although it doesn't attract the fanaticism of the Gold Wing, the big Pan European enjoys a strong worldwide following, largely as a result of its legendary longevity. It is not unusual for a 'Pan' that has been well cared for to clock up more than 400,000 km (250,000 miles) without any major engine repairs.

The engine is also unique in the world of production motorcycles, being a longitudinally mounted, double-overhead-camshaft v-four. The cylinders, angled at 90 degrees, fit neatly inside the fairing leg shields, providing the rider with a useful source of warmth in chilly weather.

Designed by Hiroshi Okazaki, the latest Pan has a sharply pointed fairing that distracts from the bulbous lines of its huge, 29-litre (6.4 gallons) fuel tank to give the impression of a motorcycle that is really rather svelte.

And it is merely an impression because, unladen, the Pan weighs in at a hefty 283 kg (624 lb). It is its bulk, however, that makes this machine such a comfortable and stable motorway-eater – although there are downsides.

The most obvious is that the bike is cumbersome to manoeuvre at low speeds and heavy to park. However, perhaps the most significant drawback of all that weight is that a hard-pressed Pan is very thirsty. Using the engine to its full potential can result in fuel consumption of as high as 8.9 kmpl (25 mpg) – not ideal in a machine designed for long-distance touring. Use the throttle gently, however, and closer to 14.2 kmpl (40 mpg) is attainable, although this is still considerably more than the rival machines of firms such as BMW and Ducati.

As is becoming the norm in the class, the Pan comes with ABS as standard, an electrically adjustable screen, colour-matched panniers and a rear luggage rack designed to take an optional top box.

Pan-European
HONDA

KAWASAKI VN1600 CLASSIC

Engine
1552 cc, liquid-cooled, fuel-injected, v-twin, four-stroke
Power
49 kW (66 bhp) @ 5000 rpm (est.)
Torque
125 Nm (92 ft lb) @ 4000 rpm
Gearbox
Five-speed
Final drive
Shaft
Weight
320 kg (705 lb)
Top speed
185 km/h (115 mph)

Kawasaki built its reputation on its high-powered superbikes such as the 900-cc Z1 of thirty years ago, but the Japanese manufacturer has also produced some impressive Harley-Davidson look-alike cruisers in its VN range.

This VN, however, belongs very firmly in the tourer class, thanks to its road-eating ability and well-appointed specification. Powered by a lazy, 1552-cc v-twin engine that produces a modest 49 kW (66 bhp), the VN1600 Classic is so understressed that it's quite likely to send its rider to sleep.

Unashamedly similar in looks to Harley-Davidson's Road King Classic, the VN matches the visual appeal of the American machine yet exceeds it in refinement. With its ultra-smooth power delivery, lack of vibration, and silky gearbox, this bike is what Harley fans might describe as "lacking in character".

The type of rider the VN is aimed at – the middle-aged, born-again biker – will doubtless be willing to sacrifice "character" for the confidence-inspiring build quality of the Kawasaki and the bullet-proof reliability of the laid-back powerplant. Check the oil and feed it petrol and the VN is almost guaranteed to take you around the world without missing a beat.

In fact, you could probably embark on a global adventure straight from the showroom thanks to the machine's useful touring equipment. While not up to Honda Gold Wing standards, it does offer a stylish screen that is entirely adequate at gentle cruising speeds, a sumptuous 'king and queen' seat with pillion backrest, and colour-matched, quickly detachable hard panniers that lend it a 1950s futuristic look.

Both rider and passenger get comfortable footboards instead of mere pegs, while the passenger also benefits from cleverly designed grab handles that are built into the panniers. And, to make sure the VN attracts as much attention as possible when a couple of hard-riding tourists pull into a new town, it sports a newly developed paint finish with an elegant, almost pebble-like sheen.

VULCAN

SPORTS BIKES

DUCATI
CORSE
DUCATI
DUCATI999
brembo

APRILIA RSV-R AND FACTORY MILLE

Engine
997 cc, liquid-cooled, double-overhead-camshaft, 60-degree v-twin, four-stroke
Power
104 kW (139 bhp) @ 9500 rpm
Torque
107 Nm (79 ft lb) @ 7500 rpm
Gearbox
Six-speed
Final drive
Chain
Weight
189 kg (417 lb) (Factory 185 kg/408 lb)
Top speed
249 km/h (155 mph) (Factory 257 km/h/160 mph)

For those to whom Italian v-twin power doesn't have to mean a Ducati, Aprilia's mighty RSV Mille has been the super-sports motorcycle of choice since it was launched in 1998; indeed, in the UK sales of the Mille are believed to outstrip those of the 999 by as much as three to one. Seven years of racing experience has benefited the bike considerably, and the latest versions are approaching the standards of reliability and build quality more often expected of the Japanese.

For 2005, the 'base model', the RSV-R, has been given revamped electronic mapping to provide greater mid-range power, although the Mille's famous tyre-shredding torque still allows it to catapult out of corners faster than almost anything else on wheels.

While still more suited to taller riders than Ducati sports bikes because of its greater seat height, the new Mille is far more compact than its famously lofty forefather but retains a distinctive look that Aprilia's designers have done well to have left alone.

Yes, there are new paint schemes, a different seat material, and an 'Air Runner' scoop at the front of the fairing, but the unusually large fuel tank makes this machine a far more practical proposition for daily use and long-distance riding than its rival.

Aprilia is also stoically refusing to follow the trend for underseat exhaust pipes, probably wisely, since that trend may be about to revert to side-mounted items following Suzuki's lead with its new GSX-R1000.

The Mille's wheels, too, remain distinctive, thanks to their slim spokes, particularly so on the race-replica version, named the Factory. This has Oz racing units to complement the various other exotic modifications that differentiate it from its standard stablemate: Ohlins suspension front and rear, an Ohlins steering damper, carbon-fibre parts, a non-slip racing seat and a black, rather than silver, frame. Both models now come equipped with radial brakes.

aprilia

aprilia
aprilia

aprilia
aprilia

BIMOTA DB5 MILLE

Engine
1000 cc, air-cooled, fuel- injected, twin-plug, l-twin, four-valve (Desmodromically operated), four-stroke
Power
70 kW (94 bhp) @ 8000 rpm
Torque
94 Nm (69 ft lb) @ 6000 rpm
Gearbox
Six-speed
Final drive
Chain
Weight
156 kg (344 lb)
Top speed
225 km/h (140 mph)

Since its founding in 1973 by the Italian motorcycle engineer and designer Massimo Tamburini, Bimota has had more than its fair share of troubles. Now, however, the famous firm – which made its name by creating exquisite, hand-built chassis to house mass-produced Japanese engines – appears to be back with a vengeance.

The DB5 Mille uses a standard Ducati 1000DS engine that hangs from a tubular chassis that can only be described as an architectural work of art. The so-called "composite trellis" rear swing arm is a first in motorcycle design and, like the rest of the frame, is painted in Italian racing red.

The aggressive, almost hawk-like, nose fairing gives way to a pair of angular lower sections that perform a suitably aerodynamic role without fully disguising the heart of the machine.

De rigueur underseat exhausts tuck in close and high at the rear, and sharp-eyed enthusiasts will recognize other components as being from the Benelli Tornado sports bike, such as the rear-view mirrors and the fairing screen.

Quality components have always been a Bimota calling card, and the DB5 Mille is no exception. The machine boasts Ohlins suspension all round and Brembo racing braking systems and, despite the relatively soft tuning of the engine, thrills are guaranteed as the entire machine weighs just 156 kg (344 lb).

In the past, another feature that marked Bimotas out from all the rest was their prohibitive price – yet, at an expected £14,000 (without tax or import duty), the DB5 Mille is actually cheaper than some of the products that the firm offered during the 1980s. It also seems a reasonable price to pay for a bike that won the Motorcycle Design Award for Best Supersport when the prototype debuted at the 2004 Intermot show.

Designer Sergio Robbiano had further cause for pride when a separate on-line poll saw the DB5 attract 15.3% of the vote, more than any other machine.

bimota
bimota

bimota

BMW
K 1200

BMW K1200 S

A pure sports BMW might sound like an oxymoron but the German manufacturer famous for its touring mounts has entered the sports-bike market with gusto.

The K1200 S is the most powerful motorcycle BMW has ever built and is intended to provide the ground-shaking performance of a focused 'hyper-sports' motorcycle with super-sport handling in a machine that is practical to ride every day.

Sounds like a tall order? Well, creating such two-wheeled perfection has clearly been a greater achievement than even BMW anticipated, because pre-production models suffered from excessive vibration, erratic idling, camshaft trouble and unpredictable high-speed handling, among other problems.

The original launch date of September 2004 was first delayed to December, at which point the first batch of 900 machines due to be distributed through European dealers was recalled without a single one being delivered, so it was well into 2005 before the first bikes hit the roads.

Among the unique features of the K1200 S is an electronic suspension system that can be adjusted while on the move by simply pressing a button on the handlebar. This innovation allows the ride to be instantly altered to suit changing surface conditions.

The all-new, in-line, four-cylinder engine has a 13:1 compression ratio – perhaps the highest ever seen on a standard production powerplant – and is capable of pushing the K1200 S to a top speed in excess of 274 km/h (170 mph) through a race-style 'cassette' gearbox that is assembled separately from the engine.

The unit also calls on race technology for its dry-sump lubrication system. This ensures a steady oil flow without the potentially damaging surges under hard cornering, acceleration and braking that are inherent in a conventional wet-sump system.

Lightweight components abound, with the alloy frame weighing just 11.5 kg (25.4 lb) and an all-new Duolever front fork achieving a weight reduction of 10% over the Telelever system used on other BMWs.

Yet, despite BMW's insistence that this is a "sports motorcycle", it is very much the company's own take on the theme. In short, this is a performance machine that places emphasis on comfort and safety and it is a world apart from the razor-sharp Japanese sports bikes to which it will unfairly be compared.

For the K1200 S is not so much aimed at racetrack refugees as at the typical, rather more thoughtful BMW rider who just happens to have a slightly rebellious streak.

Engine
1157 cc, liquid-cooled, fuel-injected, double-overhead-camshaft, in-line four-cylinder
Power
125 kW (167 bhp) @ 10,250 rpm
Torque
130 Nm (96 ft lb) @ 8250 rpm
Gearbox
Six-speed cassette unit
Final drive
Shaft
Weight
248 kg (547 lb)
Top speed
274 km/h (170 mph)

DUCATI 749 DARK

Engine
748 cc, liquid-cooled, fuel-injected, l-twin, four-valve (Desmodromically operated), four-stroke
Power
79 kW (106 bhp) @ 10,400 rpm
Torque
81 Nm (60 ft lb) @ 8500 rpm
Gearbox
Six-speed
Final drive
Chain
Weight
197 kg (434 lb)
Top speed
241 km/h (150 mph)

The new 749 Dark might be the least expensive model in Ducati's super-sports range, but it could also be one of the most important, as this is the machine designed to provide an introduction to what the firm is all about.

However, the fact that it is presented at a bargain-basement price may actually deter many buyers by making it appear to be a 'poor man's' Ducati. True, it wears a drab coat of matt-black paint and lacks the steering damper and multi-position rear monoshock of the full-specification models, but the 749 Dark has a great deal going for it.

Like its bigger, faster and more expensive 999 siblings, the latest 749 gets new fairing lower sections and a taller, more effective screen, and many people believe the engine is the sweetest of the bunch.

Less powerful, less highly tuned and consequently less harsh than the other Ducati super-sports bikes, the 749 unit can be worked harder, revved higher and used to its full potential in a way in which the larger variants often cannot because they are simply too powerful.

The 749 Dark's no-frills specification also makes it nice and light, so increasing the efficiency of the up-to-the-minute 'Testastretta' engine. This name denotes the l-twin's 'narrow head', which refers to a reduced angle between the valves that allows for a flatter combustion chamber and greater power.

The bike's light weight also ensures that the brakes are ultra-sharp and, as an added bonus, fuel economy can be pushed towards 18 kmpl (50 mpg) with careful riding. But perhaps the biggest surprise of all is that, although matt black was chosen as an economy colour scheme, it actually seems to suit the 749/999 shape more than the bolder yellow or red finishes used on the more expensive machines.

And, if you follow Henry Ford's philosophy of "any colour so long as it's black", how about the limited-edition 999S Nero shown opposite. Surely the ultimate in 'black looks'.

DUCATI999s

DUCATI749

DUCATI 999

Engine
998 cc, liquid-cooled, double-overhead-camshaft, l-twin, eight-valve, four-stroke
Power
104 kW (140 bhp) @ 9750 rpm
Torque
109 Nm (80 ft lb) @ 8000 rpm
Gearbox
Six-speed
Final drive
Chain
Weight
185 kg (408 lb)
Top speed
274 km/h (170 mph) (est.)

The latest entry-level version of the Ducati 999 comes with an engine that produces the same amount of power as the previous 'S' version, which was an expensive notch up from the standard model – yet it costs the same as the bike it replaces. Now, with 104 kW (140 bhp) on tap, the company will no doubt be hopeful that sales of the unusually styled 999 start to pick up, as the model has never matched the success of its glorious-looking predecessors, the 916, 996 and 998.

All the same, the 999 is a better machine by far: faster, better braked and, thanks to its slightly longer wheelbase, less skittish. The controversial fairing has been slightly redesigned, losing 1 kg (2¼ lb) of weight while gaining 2 cm (¾ in.) in width and a slightly taller screen intended to reduce rider fatigue at speed.

This is a machine aimed squarely at wannabe racers and, like all state-of-the-art sports bikes, it arrives virtually ready for the track, even though most will be used on the road. An extra-deep sump reduces the risk of oil starvation under the awesome acceleration of which the bike is capable, and new, higher-profile camshafts produce an extra surge of power above 6000 rpm.

If 104 kW (140 bhp) is not enough, Ducati also offers the tuned 999 'S' (107 kW/143 bhp and delivered with a race kit) and the totally track-ready 999 'R', the latest version of which makes an incredible 112 kW (150 bhp).

Those who buy a 999 for its posing power, however, may regret their choice if they do most of their riding in town. Despite the adjustable footpegs, handlebars and seat, you can only really feel comfortable on a 999 when you're hustling it around a racetrack or working the gearbox on an idyllic stretch of country road.

On the assumption that the 999 will be used as intended, it is equipped with an LCD instrument screen that incorporates a lap time recorder – although this is dominated by the considerably larger analogue rev counter mounted directly above it.

Top-quality suspension components made by Showa on the standard model and race specialists Ohlins on 'S' and 'R' versions ensure traditionally superb Ducati handling, while Brembo brakes provide pin-sharp stopping power.

The basic model comes with a pillion seat, which is an option on the 'S', but 'R' models are supplied strictly 'monoposto'.

DUCATI SUPERBIKE
marchesini

HONDA CBR 600RR

Engine
599 cc, liquid-cooled, double-overhead-camshaft, in-line four-cylinder, four-stroke
Power
86 kW (115 bhp) @ 13,000 rpm
Torque
Not available
Gearbox
Six-speed
Final drive
Chain
Weight
163 kg (359 lb)
Top speed
257 km/h (160 mph)

Honda's CBR 600 has been the benchmark in middleweight sports bikes for years – but this is an area of motorcycle production in which no manufacturer can afford to rest on its laurels, such is the intensity of competition and the speed of development.

Intended as the basis for Honda's assault on the current World Supersport race series, the road-going CBR 600RR is 6 kg (13.2 lb) lighter than the model it replaces. The manufacturer has shed weight wherever possible, even shaving 64 g (2.3 oz) from the fuel-injection nozzles and producing an entirely new 'fine die cast' frame in order to trim off just 1.5 kg (3.3 lb).

Power output remains the same as last year – but a better power-to-weight ratio translates to better outright performance, meaning the new machine is harder accelerating and more responsive. It also has a built-in 'overrev' ability, which allows it to be race-tuned so that it produces more power higher in the rev range. This is done by making a simple adjustment to the electronic control unit (ECU).

Honda's current aim for its sports bikes is to centralize as much weight as possible, by lightening the front and rear ends and concentrating the mass low down in the middle of the machine. However, the aggressive, mid-mounted exhaust nestling beneath the CBR 600's seat tail has less to do with centralization than cool looks, pure and simple.

The fact is, most 600-cc sports bikes are bought by relatively recently qualified riders who are eager to look as though they are riding to work on Monday morning after a hard weekend at the racetrack.

Part of the genius of Honda's engineers is that machines such as the CBR 600RR are actually fast enough and nimble enough to battle it out on the world's circuits yet tractable and reliable enough to be used for the daily commute.

But this does not mean that they are practical for this purpose, even if the minimal space beneath the CBR's seat is specifically designed to accommodate an optional security lock. The machine's ergonomic arrangement requires the rider to adopt a racing crouch, the passenger must sit on a thin pad set somewhat higher than the main seat, and, for the sake of compactness and reduced weight, the fuel tank offers a rather limited range.

HONDA

HONDA

HONDA

Arai

ZX-6R
Kawasaki
Ninja
636

Kawasaki's ZX-6 has never provided much competition for the middleweight sports bikes of Honda, Suzuki and Yamaha – until now.

Ironically, Kawasaki can lay claim to establishing the class with the introduction of the GPZ 600R more than twenty years ago, yet of late its products have enjoyed a relatively small share of the market in what has become a highly important and competitive area.

The last ZX-6R, however, made the world sit up and take notice – but that, it seems, was a mere taster for the surprise that came with the latest C1 model. Not only is this the most aerodynamic motorcycle Kawasaki has ever produced, it is aggressively attractive all the way from the dominant, central air intake between the headlights to the subtle, oval exhaust that protrudes from beneath the LED tail light.

Its crankshaft power output leaves the competition standing, measuring 95 kW (128 bhp) at a heady 14,000 rpm. This translates to around 11 kW (15 bhp) more power at the rear wheel than is produced by the Honda CBR 600RR, the Kawasaki's deadly rival.

Considerable thought has been put into the ergonomics of the machine, too, following criticism of its predecessor for being too racetrack-orientated and therefore impractical for normal road use. While the classic sports-bike riding position is needed, the footrests are not positioned so far back as to make city use uncomfortable, the seat is unusually wide, and the rear suspension provides the magical combination of comfort and sharp handling, thanks to its adjustability.

This is linked to the now-fashionable braced aluminium swing arm, finished in the same satin black as the frame and lower fairing, while a back torque limiter – which prevents the rear wheel from locking during downward gear changes at high revs – and competition-style 'petal' brake discs with radial calipers add to the ZX-6R's competition credentials.

If the standard version fails to meet your racing aspirations, however, a limited-edition 'RR' model is also available. Designed first and foremost for racetrack use, it has a performance-tuned exhaust system and altered electronic mapping to provide more power and higher revs.

KAWASAKI ZX-6R C1

Engine
636 cc, fuel-injected, double-overhead-camshaft, four-cylinder, sixteen-valve, four-stroke
Power
95 kW (128 bhp) @ 14,000 rpm
Torque
66 Nm (49 ft lb) @ 10,000 rpm
Gearbox
Six-speed with back torque limiter clutch
Final drive
Chain
Weight
164 kg (362 lb)
Top speed
265 km/h (165 mph)

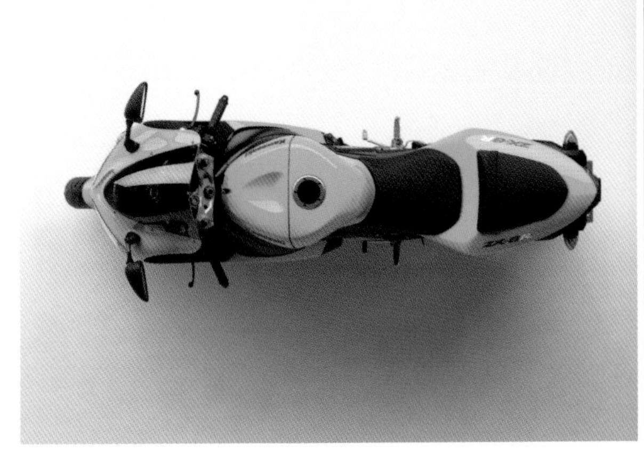

MOTO GUZZI MGS-01 CORSA

Engine
1256 cc, air-cooled, 90-degree v-twin, four-stroke
Power
91 kW (122 bhp) @ 8000 rpm
Torque
12 Nm (8 ft lb) @ 6400 rpm
Gearbox
Six-speed
Final drive
Shaft
Weight
192 kg (423 lb)
Top speed
241 km/h (150 mph)

The original Moto Guzzi Le Mans of the late 1970s was regarded by many as one of the most handsome sports motorcycles of all time. Long, low and lean, it just begged to be ridden hard and fast.

A Le Mans model is still very much part of the modern Moto Guzzi line-up, but it is not a sports bike in the league of Ducati's 999 or Aprilia's RSV Mille – the MGS-01, however, certainly is.

This gorgeous-looking track machine is the fruit of a 'style laboratory' set up by Guzzi in 2002 to capitalize on the skills and creativity of celebrated Italian custom-bike designers, among them the legendary duo of Ghezzi and Brian.

The best human and technical resources were made available for the project and, less than nine months after first putting pen to paper, Ghezzi and Brian came up with a presentable show bike that wowed the crowds at that year's Intermot in Munich.

Ride, handling and performance were what the MGS-01 was to be all about, so it was given a short wheelbase, superb balance and top-quality ancillary components. The 1256-cc engine features four-valve cylinder heads, three-ring Cosworth racing pistons and ceramic-coated cylinder bores.

With a tuning kit available to bring power up to 91 kW (122 bhp) and an all-up weight of just 192 kg (423 lb) – distributed almost perfectly, with a difference of just 200 g (7 oz) between front and back – the MGS-01 is a serious track tool. The uncompromising nature of this machine is further demonstrated by the radially mounted Brembo racing brakes and the Ohlins suspension at front and rear.

The first batch of MGS-01 machines – designated 'Corsa' models – has already been released for track use and hopes are high that the long-awaited homologated, street-legal 'Serie' version will be made available in the near future. If it is, there will be no shortage of buyers.

TERMIGNONI
GUZZI

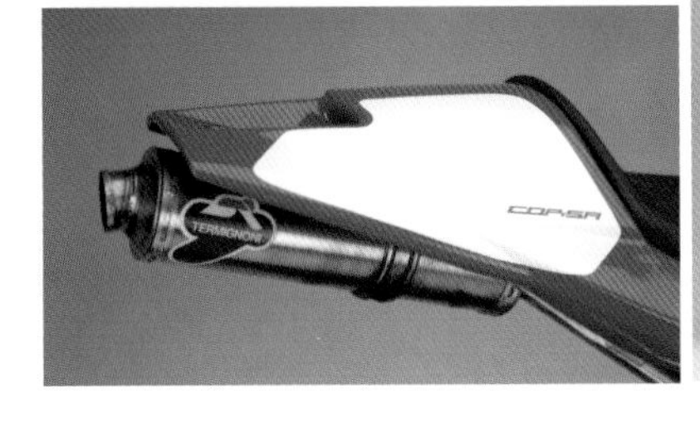
CORSA

brembo
ÖHLINS

MV AGUSTA F4 1000 AGO

Engine
996 cc, liquid-cooled, in-line four-cylinder, four-stroke
Power
124 kW (166 bhp) @ 11,750 rpm
Torque
109 Nm (80 ft lb) @ 10,200 rpm
Gearbox
Six-speed cassette unit
Final drive
Chain
Weight
190 kg (419 lb)
Top speed
301 km/h (187 mph)

It is fitting that, exactly sixty years after it was founded in 1945, the Italian firm of MV Agusta should produce a special machine in tribute to its most famous – if not the world's most famous – motorcycle racer.

Giacomo Agostini was recruited by Count Domenico Agusta to ride for the MV team in 1965. In a seventeen-year career with MV Agusta, 'Ago' went on to win no fewer than fourteen world titles, ten Isle of Man TT races and 250 other events around the globe – more victories than any other rider in the history of motorcycling.

No wonder, then, that MV has pulled out all the stops in the creation of its stunning tribute bike, the F4 1000 Ago. Producing an awesome 124 kW (166 bhp) at 11,750 rpm, the machine has a top speed of 301 km/h (187 mph) and weighs a mere 190 kg (419 lb).

Despite its twenty-first-century sophistication, the Ago bears an eerie resemblance to Agostini's track bikes of the 1960s and 1970s. It has the same seat upholstered in red Alcantara; the rider's famous "1" on yellow roundels is seen on the fairing; and the colour scheme is, of course, the MV factory livery of red and silver.

Instrumentation is dominated by a large, white tachometer with blue gradations, at the bottom of which is a facsimile of Agostini's signature, and an eighteen-carat-gold plate inside the fairing marks out each of these limited-edition machines as being something very special indeed.

As a finishing touch the Italian *tricolore* appears on either side of the tailpiece directly above those four delicious 'organ pipe' exhausts.

However, as the performance figures indicate, this machine is not merely a sentimental tribute of the "all show and no go" variety: it is equipped with the finest racing components, such as Nissin brakes, Marchesini wheels, a Sachs competition monoshock and track-specification Showa forks. The quick-change cassette gearbox comes directly from the Cagiva factory race bikes (Cagiva now owns the MV marque) and the bike also boasts a unique engine braking system (EBS) that reduces the risk of wheel locking during hard downshifts through the gears.

If ever there was an instant classic in the making, the MV F4 1000 Ago is it.

AGO
CRC
AGUSTA
1

AGO
CRC
AGUSTA
1

MV AGUSTA F4 1000 TAMBURINI

Engine
998 cc, liquid-cooled, in-line four-cylinder with radial valves, four-stroke
Power
129 kW (173 bhp) @ 11,750 rpm
Torque
113 Nm (83 ft lb) @ 9200 rpm
Gearbox
Six-speed cassette unit
Final drive
Chain
Weight
184 kg (406 lb)
Top speed
306 km/h (190 mph)

As exotic as MV Agusta's F4 1000 Ago is, there are some enthusiasts for whom it is just not exclusive enough – and these are the people who are expected to order the ultra-limited-edition F4 1000 Tamburini.

Named after its creator Massimo Tamburini, the legendary motorcycle designer who penned the iconic lines of the Ducati 916, the F4 Tamburini is one of the most expensive motorcycles ever produced by a volume manufacturer: it costs more than £28,000.

For their money, the few lucky buyers will get a machine bristling with extremely high-quality componentry and upgrades, including a unique and patented, variable-length air-intake arrangement that MV is calling 'TSS', for 'torque shift system'.

This, along with the use of lightweight engine internals, will boost the already impressive power of the F4 1000-cc engine to 129 kW (173 bhp) while enabling it to make more torque at lower revs. An increase of 5 kW (7 bhp) over the standard (124 kW/166 bhp) unit may not sound much, but it represents a significant performance boost, thanks to the fact that the Tamburini weighs 6 kg (13 lb) less than the 'ordinary' machine.

The F4 Tamburini is far more of a motorcycle than any road rider could realistically need – but the reason for its existence is to make a statement. It is an experiment in creating two-wheeled perfection that goes beyond the boundaries of what has ever been made before.

Sadly, however, rare, beautiful and expensive motorcycles such as this are seldom used to the full: some will undoubtedly end up in museum collections, others will probably take pride of place as rolling artworks in their owner's houses and others will be locked away in hermetically sealed containers until they have risen in value sufficiently to be sold on.

As a result, the chances of seeing one on the road are decidedly slim – particularly on a rainy day.

AGUSTA
F4

Tamburini
F4
CRC

SUZUKI GSX-R1000

It was in 1985 that Suzuki unleashed the original GSX-R 'hyper-sports' 750 to establish the trend for race-replica motorcycles that continues today.

The blue-and-white finish of those early machines is still regarded as the classic GSX-R colour scheme, so, to mark two decades of what has become a legend, Suzuki has used it to dress a special twentieth-anniversary GSX-R750.

But the latest one litre 'Gixxer', shown here, is light years ahead of its forefathers, boasting a 999-cc engine that is said to yield 112 kW (150 bhp). In order to reaffirm its position at the top of the sports-bike tree, Suzuki has lightened, redesigned, and tweaked the previous sharp-handling and amazingly fast GSX-R1000 into a machine that represents a benchmark for its class.

Almost all its individual components, from the lightweight wheels and subframe to the pure titanium valves, have been trimmed to the bone to save weight. The pistons, for example, collectively save 32 g (1.1 oz) by being 1.5 mm (0.05 in.) shorter and 8.9 mm (0.4 in.) narrower than those on the old model. In the super-sports class, these things really count.

The GSX-R1000's aerodynamics have also been improved by incorporating the front indicators into the mirrors and the rear ones into an unusual, bulbous tailpiece, while the machine as a whole has been made narrower, shorter, and more squat in order to lessen the frontal area and lower the centre of gravity. The motorcycle's dimensions are, in fact, more in keeping with a 600-cc model.

A trapezoidal radiator makes for increased cooling capacity without increased size, a race-type 'slipper' clutch is fitted and, while the opposition is still busy perfecting the underseat exhaust styling first used by Ducati, Suzuki is very much doing its own thing.

Rather than follow the crowd, the 'Big S' has chosen to endow the GSX-R with a chunky, triangular, upswept exhaust can that hangs from the right-hand pillion footrest mount in the 'old-fashioned' way. Again made from titanium, the lightweight Suzuki Advanced Exhaust System (SAES) has been pulled in as tightly as possible to the bike's centre of gravity to help handling and improve ground clearance.

All in all, this looks like the ultimate sports bike, although it will, of course, be quickly bettered – if not by Suzuki itself, then by one of its three rivals. It will be interesting to see who follows the leader with another take on the side-mounted, triangular exhaust.

Engine
999 cc, liquid-cooled, fuel-injected, double-overhead-camshaft, four-cylinder, four-stroke
Power
112 kW (150 bhp) @ 11,000 rpm
Torque
118 (87 ft lb) @ 8300 rpm
Gearbox
Six-speed
Final drive
Chain
Weight
166 kg (366 lb)
Top speed
298 km/h (185 mph)

RIZLA+
Q8 Oils
SUZUKI
72
SUZUKI
TITANIUM
SUZUKI
SUZUKI

TRIUMPH DAYTONA 650

Engine
646 cc, liquid-cooled, fuel-injected, double-overhead-camshaft, four-cylinder, four-stroke
Power
73 kW (98 bhp) @ 12,500 rpm
Torque
68 Nm (50 ft lb) @ 11,500 rpm
Gearbox
Six-speed with backlash eliminator gear
Final drive
Chain
Weight
165 kg (364 lb)
Top speed
257 km/h (160 mph)

The still-young Triumph company – revived from the dead by businessman John Bloor in the early 1990s – is both big enough to take on the Japanese giants in the ultra-competitive middleweight sports class and clever enough to give them serious cause for concern.

Styling-wise, Triumph has opted for a distinctive, angular look that sets the bike apart from the opposition, while this latest model features an enlarged cylinder capacity, created by increasing piston stroke 3.1 mm (0.1 in.) to give an extra 47 cc.

Triumph's original attempt at a middleweight sports bike, the TT600, was heavily criticized for the poor performance of its EFi fuel-injection system, which resulted in patchy delivery and irritating flat spots. It is a legacy that has, rather unfairly, blighted later versions too. To put this devil to rest, Triumph has significantly reworked the tuning of the EFi and now promises "lightning throttle response" and super-smooth power delivery.

One feature of the old 600-cc models that could never be criticized, however, was their handling, and this has been carried over to the Daytona 650 in an ultra-rigid, ultra-light aluminium, twin-spar frame constructed from three separate 'cells'.

All-aluminium front forks are among the lightest in their class, while the bike's short wheelbase – just 139 cm (54.7 in.) – makes for super-quick steering and supreme 'flickability'.

On paper, therefore, the Daytona 650 looks like it should at least match, or even outsell, the opposition. In fact, however, this is merely a stop-gap model, as Triumph is now putting the finishing touches to a radical, new middleweight super-sports bike, a 680-cc triple-cylinder machine.

Perhaps this will be the bike that Triumph uses to get its name back on to the racetrack to achieve some serious results. At the moment the firm's sports bikes are seriously lacking in street cred among the type of motorcyclists who should be buying them. And that means everyone is missing out.

TRIUMPH
Daytona

TRIUMPH
Daytona

YAMAHA R6

Race results, an impressive competition history and having a big brother as successful as the 1000-cc R1 have all helped Yamaha's R6 to become one of the most popular of the middleweight sports bikes. So why change a recipe that works?

Yamaha could not, of course, simply re-present the old R6, for fear of being accused of offering a stale product, however good it was. Instead, the Japanese giant has endowed the latest version of the bike with an extra 2 kW (3 bhp) through the use of enlarged throttle bodies, increased the size of the brakes to 31 cm (12.2 in.) and slimmed them down to save weight.

In keeping with modern trends, the new R6 has inverted front forks and the wheelbase has been stretched by 5 mm (0.2 in.) for added stability. And, as if to prove that Yamaha listens to its customers, the R6 now comes with a slightly wider front tyre, just like the one many 'real world' riders said worked best.

These, together with a range of new colour schemes, are just the type of small changes that suggest a totally reworked R6 is in the pipeline. If so, the chances are it will be considerably more radical, to trump the likes of Honda's CBR 600RR and Kawasaki's ZX-6.

If a top speed of 257 km/h (160 mph), taut, predictable handling and a surprising level of in-town comfort are features in a motorcycle that appeal to you, the latest R6 might just be an ideal buy – assuming you can live with a bike that is not nearly as trendy as it once was. However, it might be wise to wait until the next-generation version is revealed, as that way you can haggle for a bargain.

Engine
599 cc, liquid-cooled, fuel-injected, double-overhead-camshaft, four-cylinder, four-stroke
Power
94 kW (126 bhp) @ 13,000 rpm
Torque
66 Nm (49 ft lb) @ 12,000 rpm
Gearbox
Six-speed
Final drive
Chain
Weight
163 kg (359 lb)
Top speed
257 km/h (160 mph)

YAMAHA

YAMAHA

R1200ST

SPORTS TOURERS

BMW R1200 ST

Not since the mid-1980s has BMW used the designation "ST" to describe one of its models. Back then it was on the unusual-looking R80 ST, a strange machine based on BMW's GS trail bike and fitted with road-orientated tyres and suspension.

The new ST is nothing like that, however. It is a thoroughly modern, 241-km/h (150 mph) motorcycle that goes a long way to fulfilling the inevitably compromised role of 'sports tourer'.

At first sight the most striking aspect of the ST is its sharply angled, twin headlamp fairing. This contrives to be both sporty and practical thanks to an electric screen that complements a seat and handlebars that are both height-adjustable.

To give the ST a performance edge over the R1200 RT pure tourer model, it has been trimmed of 17 kg (37.5 lb) of weight and endowed with a tuned version of the RT's classic BMW flat-twin 'boxer' engine, which provides an extra 11 kW (15 bhp).

However, the fuel tank, with its capacity of 20.9 litres (4.6 gallons), still allows a potential range of 480 km (300 miles). And to ensure a suitable level of comfort when the bike is used in a touring rather than a 'sports' role (as, more often than not, it will be), various accessories are available, including ABS, heated grips and an entirely new, waterproof pannier system.

Engine
1170 cc, air-cooled, flat-twin, eight-valve, four-stroke
Power
93 kW (125 bhp) @ 7500 rpm
Torque
115 Nm (85 ft lb) @ 6000 rpm
Gearbox
Six-speed
Final drive
Shaft
Weight
242 kg (534 lb)
Top speed
241 km/h (150 mph)

DUCATI ST4s/ ST4s ABS

Engine
996 cc, liquid-cooled, l-twin, three valves (Desmodromically operated) per cylinder, four-stroke
Power
90 kW (121 bhp) @ 8750 rpm
Torque
103 Nm (76 ft lb) @ 7250 rpm
Gearbox
Six-speed
Final drive
Chain
Weight
205 kg (452 lb) (210 kg/463 lb with ABS)
Top speed
233 km/h (145 mph)

Ducati motorcycles are perceived first and foremost as uncompromising sports machines, but the latest ST4s model is undoubtedly designed for comfortable long-distance travel and, as such, belongs firmly in the sports-touring category.

This bike eats up the road with relish, thanks to the 90-kW (121 bhp) engine inherited directly from the legendary 996 race replica. Rider comfort is increased by the provision of height-adjustable handlebars while, on the top-of-the-range model, safety is enhanced through the addition of a newly developed anti-lock braking system.

To cater for the differing load weights commonly carried by touring motorcycles, the ST4s offers numerous front- and rear-suspension settings, a direct inheritance from Ducati's sports-bike class, which is fabled for its superb handling.

Adding to the refinement of the machine is a new, oil-bath clutch that overcomes the characteristic Ducati clatter at tick-over (and which should enhance reliability, a vital factor on a hard-pressed touring machine). The ST4s is also the first motorcycle to feature a data display that receives information via the Controller Area Network (CAN), a type of technology previously only seen in the car industry.

Touring riders with an allegiance to the type of machines produced by BMW or Honda might not give the Ducati a second thought as a potential mount for a two-wheeled odyssey. But those who do will discover a highly capable machine with an irresistible character.

They will also appreciate two distinct features of the ST4s that set it apart from other motorcycles in the category. The first is its low weight – 205 kg (452 lb) against, say, the 377 kg (831 lb) of the Harley-Davidson Electra Glide – which, combined with Ducati's famous trellis frame, enables the ST4s to be flicked through the switchbacks with ease even when fully laden. The second is its deliciously 'grunty' engine, which punches the bike out of corners from the lowest of revs yet can be wound up to give a top speed of over 225 km/h (140 mph).

You won't get off the ST4s after a hard day in the saddle feeling anywhere near as fresh as if you had been on a Honda Gold Wing, but you'll undoubtedly feel you've bonded with your machine and enjoy a keen sense of having really travelled.

DUCATI
ST4s
DUCATI
ST3

DUCATI
ST4s

MZ

MZ

MZ 1000S

MZ has made a bold move in launching its 1000S in the competitive sports-touring market dominated by makers such as Honda, Yamaha, Triumph and Ducati. But the German firm should be applauded for creating a totally fresh look rather than following the crowd.

The slab-sided fairing has a distinctly '1970s futuristic' look, while the fuel tank and seat unit abound with sharp angles. Everything has a slight air of being built down to a price and the overall construction quality fails to match that of the competition, but riders looking for something different may accept this as part of the MZ's character.

The 1000S also uses a somewhat outmoded parallel-twin-cylinder engine – a configuration not available in any other large-capacity sports tourer. This doesn't perform well at low revs, particularly compared with the torquey v-twin of a Ducati, for example.

Higher up the rev range, however, the liquid-cooled twin proves surprisingly powerful, with around 87 kW (117 bhp) available at the crankshaft, good enough for a top speed of 225 km/h (140 mph).

MZ claims the wheels used on the 1000S are uniquely light, and these 17-in. (43.2 cm), cast-alloy items do have a 10% weight advantage over conventional wheels. Such a saving of unsprung weight helps create generally neutral handling characteristics, although the bike can become skittish on poorly surfaced roads.

The speedometer and tachometer are refreshingly conventional analog units, while an LCD distance meter, trip meter and clock are built into the binnacle to the side. Unusually for a tourer, there is no fuel gauge.

Engine
998 cc, liquid-cooled, double-overhead-camshaft, parallel-twin, eight-valve, four-stroke

Power
87 kW (117 bhp) @ 9000 rpm

Torque
95 Nm (70 ft lb) @ 7000 rpm

Gearbox
Six-speed

Final drive
Chain

Weight
210 kg (463 lb)

Top speed
225 km/h (140 mph)

TRIUMPH SPRINT ST

Engine
1050 cc, fuel-injected, double-overhead-camshaft, three-cylinder, four-stroke
Power
93 kW (125 bhp) @ 9000 rpm
Torque
104 Nm (77 ft lb) @ 5000 rpm
Gearbox
Six-speed
Final drive
Chain
Weight
210kg (463 lb)
Top speed
249 km/h (155 mph)

If ever there was a nondescript motorcycle it was the old version of Triumph's Sprint ST sports tourer, a machine created from a bland mix of stodgy styling, indifferent performance and little character that somehow established a loyal following.

Before the wraps were removed from this entirely new Sprint ST, many people were expecting more of the same – but they were in for a shock. Triumph's design team has been working overtime to produce a svelte beauty with features to make any rider of a pure sports machine envious.

The triple theme inspired by Triumph's famous three-cylinder engine configuration is carried through to the rest of the bike in areas such as the three-light fairing, the cluster of three instruments and the trio of underseat exhaust pipes.

To match the stylish new image, engine capacity has been upped from 955 cc to 1050 cc and softly tuned for touring purposes. The engine is carried in an entirely new aluminium frame that gives a relatively short wheelbase for this category of bike, enabling it to turn more quickly.

The rear end is slightly 'jacked up' to enhance the Sprint ST's sporty nature and the machine has the handling and performance to match, making it a definite contender for the title of best all-rounder, a position currently held, as widely agreed, by Honda's VFR 800, which now looks rather dated in comparison.

And, not forgetting this bike is as much 'tourer' as 'sports', Triumph made available from launch a comprehensive range of luggage for the Sprint ST, including a three-box pannier system with detachable, soft inner bags, an extra-comfortable gel seat and an aero screen. Other optional extras are throw-over saddlebags, a shaped tank bag and satellite navigation.

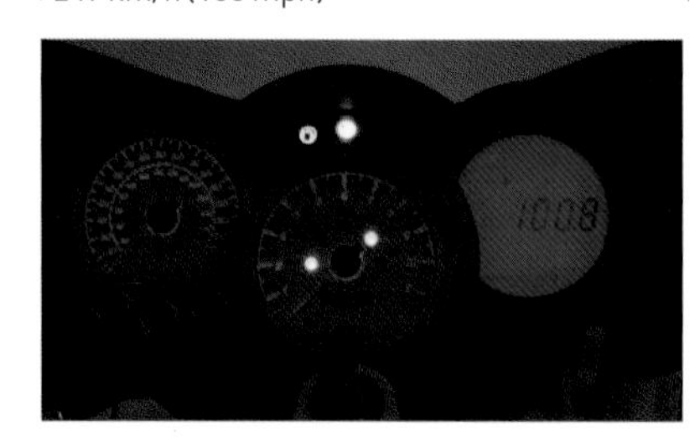

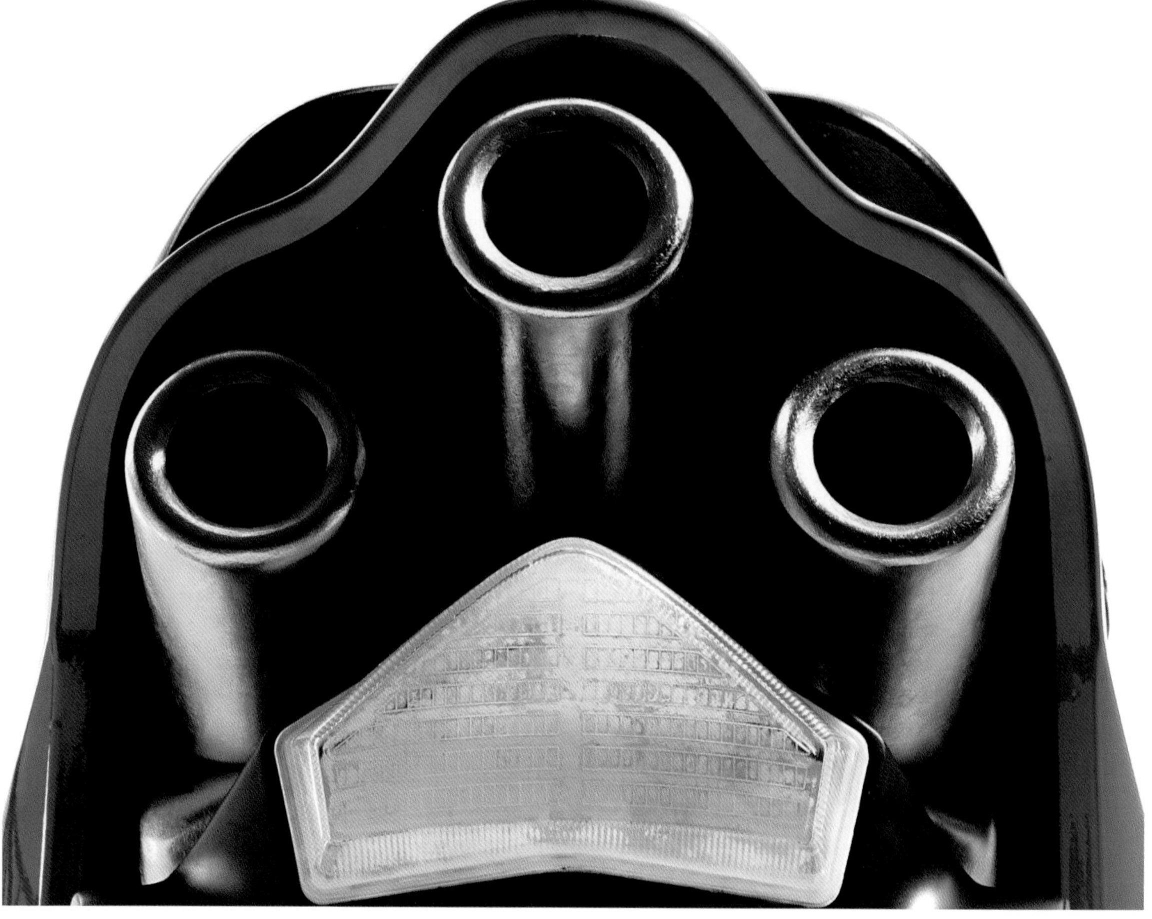

TRIUMPH
SPRINT
ST
1050

TRIUMPH
SPRINT
ST
1050

YAMAHA FJR1300

It is more than twenty years since Yamaha accidentally created the ancestor of what is now regarded as one of the most capable sports tourers on the market. Back then the FJ1100 was a chain-drive machine that was originally built as a high-speed 'pure sports' bike.

The fact that it was not only fast but large, comfortable, quiet and docile when required meant riders quickly discovered that the first FJ was also a superb machine for touring. Therefore, rather than try to spice up its sporty nature, Yamaha went with the flow and, through the next-generation FJ1200, further enhanced the model's touring abilities.

Production of the original FJ range ceased in the 1990s, but in 2001 Yamaha returned to the sports-tourer market with the all-new FJR1300, which had all the distance-consuming capabilities of the old bike but with far sweeter handling and even better performance.

Light, quick and technologically advanced, the 2005 FJR1300 is the sportiest of the line and borrows several features from Yamaha's YZF race replica, such as its 'cat's eye' headlamps and pin-sharp brakes.

A smooth, aerodynamic look has been achieved with a one-piece unit combining rear light and turn signal, while the front indicators are smoothly blended into the large and highly effective fairing, which has an electrically adjustable screen.

A 30-litre (6.6 gallons) tank (made from steel to enable a magnetic bag to be attached) ensures that the big FJR can cruise for as much as 480 km (300 miles) between fill-ups.

Other touring touches include a driveshaft integral with the swing arm, a seat made from foam of varying density for ultimate rider and passenger comfort and a quick-release, one-key luggage system.

And, despite its considerable weight, the FJR can be thrown around with gusto, thanks to an ultra-light, twin-spar frame made from hollow cast aluminium that uses the engine as a fully stressed member. To enhance touring safety there is the option of ABS braking.

As *Cycle World* said when naming the FJR1300 sports tourer of the year: "with superb luggage, superbike power, fine handling and great riding position, nothing can touch it for eating all the pavement you care to feed it at a rate that will embarrass any other bike with saddlebags."

Engine
1298 cc, liquid-cooled, double-overhead-camshaft, sixteen-valve, four-stroke
Power
108 kW (145 bhp) @ 8500 rpm
Torque
134 Nm (99 ft lb) @ 7000 rpm
Gearbox
Five-speed
Final drive
Shaft
Weight
244 kg (537 lb) (ABS version 251 kg/553 lb)
Top speed
257 km/h (160 mph)

STREET, NAKED AND MUSCLE

APRILIA TUONO

Engine
997 cc, liquid-cooled, 60-degree v-twin, four-stroke
Power
84 kW (112 bhp) @ 7000 rpm
Torque
95 Nm (70 ft lb) @ 6500 rpm
Gearbox
Six-speed
Final drive
Chain
Weight
191 kg (421 lb)
Top speed
248 km/h (154 mph)

Aprilia's lusty Tuono is the epitome of the naked street bike. It's essentially the RSV Mille with the sports handlebars and racing fairing replaced by a fly screen and a more upright riding position.

As a result, it is just about the fastest naked on the road, offering a top speed of 248 km/h (154 mph) if you're strong enough to hang on in the wind blast. This is a raw and aggressive machine that is loud, brash and fabulous fun.

Wheelies are available in the first three gears with the merest tweak of the throttle, and the racing Brembo disc brakes will stand this 191-kg (421 lb) lightweight on its nose with ease. At the same time, it has inherited the on-rails handling of its race-replica sibling and can confidently be leaned over at seemingly impossible angles.

Somewhat taller than the competition, the Tuono is surprisingly comfortable on the type of longer journeys to which naked bikes are not generally suited. However, the huge power and urgency of the engine make it something of a handful when used for the town riding that nakeds are supposed to be so good for.

Compared with its more radical competitors, such as Triumph's Speed Triple and Benelli's TNT, the Tuono looks conventional and almost old-fashioned, but it has bang-up-to-date components, a super-powerful engine, and, best of all, the least expensive price tag of any 1000-cc street bike. How can it fail?

aprilia racing
aprilia

aprilia
aprilia

aprilia
aprilia racing
aprilia

BENELLI TNT SPORT/ TITANIUM/CAFÉ RACER

Engine
1130 cc, liquid-cooled, adjustable-fuel-injection, double-overhead-camshaft, three-cylinder, four-stroke
Power
104 kW (139 bhp) @ 9250 rpm
Torque
117 Nm (86 ft lb) @ 6750 rpm
Gearbox
Six-speed
Final drive
Chain
Weight
199 kg (439 lb)
Top speed
249 km/h (155 mph)

Benelli's mean-looking nakeds have an almost insect-like quality that makes them seem as though they have hatched from an alien egg rather than been developed by CAD in a motorcycle design studio.

The new TNT Sport builds on the recently launched standard model by offering enhanced handling through multi-adjustable Marzocchi forks and an Extreme Technology rear monoshock. The Sport also gets race-style radial brakes, apparently an improvement prompted by feedback from customers who were not just using their TNTs as posing machines but riding them as hard and fast as they were intended to be.

This is certainly no machine for shrinking violets: it grabs attention wherever it stops, with its bright-red frame, black paintwork and bronze-anodized forks, handlebars and disc centres.

It offers an interesting technological advance, too, in the inclusion of a handlebar-adjustable system that enables the rider to change the mapping of the fuel injection at the flick of a switch.

On the 'controlled power' setting, a quarter of the engine's potential power is suppressed for a smoother delivery in slow-speed, commuter situations; reset the switch to 'free power' and all of the TNT's considerable potential can be released for the open road.

As well as the Sport model, the TNT is available in a super-exclusive variant called the Titanium that has forged-alloy Marchesini racing wheels, a full complement of carbon-fibre bodywork, titanium exhaust pipes and the complex, multi-adjustable suspension from the Tornado sports bike on which all TNTs are based.

The model may also become available as the Café Racer, a 'concept' version of which has been created using low-mounted, clip-on handlebars, a single seat and numerous carbon-fibre components.

brembo
D208F

BIMOTA TESI 2D

Almost since the first motorcycles travelled down a rutted road under their own power, designers have been looking for the ideal way in which to attach a front wheel and make it go exactly where you point it.

The telescopic fork is generally regarded as the best solution and has been more or less in universal use for three quarters of a century. Nevertheless, engineers continue to be niggled by the fact that even the most substantial fork legs have a tendency to flex under hard cornering, and it doesn't take a mathematician to work out that the steering geometry of the motorcycle is severely altered every time they compress.

Many people believe the solution lies in 'hub-centre' steering, where the front wheel is attached by a suitably modified, articulated version of the swing-arm suspension more commonly found at the back of a bike.

Yamaha was the first major manufacturer to produce a machine with hub-centre steering, the GTS 1000, but the firm that is most famous for experimenting with the idea is the Italian frame specialist Bimota. Sadly, this is largely because the Tesi 1D, which appeared in 1991, proved such a spectacular failure that it sapped the company of what little cash it had.

Undaunted by this earlier setback, the revived Bimota has announced that it will produce the Tesi 2D ('*tesi*' is Italian for 'thesis'). Only around thirty-five machines will be built per year, with a suitably exclusive price tag of around £23,000.

They will be powered by the same Ducati 1000DS engine used in Bimota's DB5 Mille, but the rest of the motorcycle is very different: the frame, for example, is milled from solid aircraft aluminium with a giant, triangular-section swing arm, and the mechanics of the hub-centre steering have produced an extraordinary, hawk-like appearance.

The exhaust hangs low directly beneath the centre of the engine, Buell-style, but it is somewhat unusual in that the exit pipe is found towards the front of the machine rather than at the rear.

It seems inevitable that the Tesi 2D's exclusivity will ensure that it sells, but whether or not the world of mainstream motorcycling is yet ready for hub-centre steering, almost fifteen years after Bimota's first attempt, remains a matter for conjecture.

Engine
991 cc, air-cooled, twin-plug, l-twin, four-stroke
Power
64 kW (86 bhp) @ 8000 rpm
Torque
88 Nm (65 ft lb) @ 6300 rpm
Gearbox
Six-speed
Final drive
Chain
Weight
149 kg (328 lb)
Top speed
225 km/h (140 mph)

BMW K1200 R

Engine
1157 cc, liquid-cooled, fuel-injected, double-overhead-camshaft, four-cylinder, four-stroke
Power
119 kW (160 bhp) @ 10,250 rpm
Torque
125 Nm (92 ft lb) @ 8250 rpm
Gearbox
Five-speed
Final drive
Chain
Weight
220 kg (485 lb)
Top speed
257 km/h (160 mph)

Considering that most people regard BMWs as being machines for the sensible, the firm is surprisingly good at coming up with off-the-wall creations.

A couple of years ago BMW's designers went on a parts-bin raid and attached a headlamp unit from the R1150 GS trail bike to the front of a naked 1150 R flat-twin tourer to produce a street bike named the Rockster.

Now they've repeated the trick, this time using the phenomenally powerful four-cylinder engine from the K1200 sports bike as the basis for a 'naked', to which they have added a small, Perspex screen and the headlamps and instrument binnacle from the R1200 GS.

The street-fighter look is completed by the addition of motocross-style handlebars that work through an altered steering-head angle to give quicker direction changes, a 'muscular' 19-litre (4.2 gallons) fuel tank and a tail section designed to mark it out from other BMWs.

The result is a mean-looking motorcycle that, incidentally, also has an extremely high power output for a machine in this category – it is said to produce 119 kW (160 bhp). Despite driving through a lower final-drive ratio than the sporty K1200 S does, this should endow the un-faired K1200 R with a theoretical top speed in excess of 257 km/h (160 mph). Hang on if you dare.

METZELER
Castrol
LASER

Castrol
METZELER
LASER
BMW

BUELL LIGHTNING CITY XB9SX

Engine
984 cc, air-, oil- and fan-cooled, 45-degree v-twin, four-stroke
Power
63 kW (84 bhp) @ 6600 rpm
Torque
86 Nm (63 ft lb) @ 5600 rpm
Gearbox
Five-speed
Final drive
Belt
Weight
175 kg (386 lb)
Top speed
209 km/h (130 mph)

Buell's Lightning City XB9SX is neither the fastest nor the most powerful naked street bike on the market, but it is certainly one of the most interesting in terms of design.

Created primarily for two-wheeled combat in the urban jungle, it features a tuned and fuel-injected Harley-Davidson engine in the unique Buell chassis configuration. This comprises a simple-looking but incredibly rigid and massively constructed, twin-spar aluminium frame attached to a very short, stiff swing arm through a Showa monoshock.

Integral to the Buell philosophy is a low centre of gravity, so the Lightning City XB9SX carries its 14 litres (3 gallons) of fuel inside its frame and one side of the swing arm doubles as an oil reservoir.

The single colour scheme of black and blue has been chosen for both practical and aesthetic reasons. The Villain Black cast-aluminium wheels and Midnight Black bellypan are so coloured to defeat city grime, while blue is used for the instrument gauge faces and backlights, the perforated tail insert, the minimal Perspex screen and, most significantly, on what we would expect to be the fuel tank.

Since the Buell stores its fuel in the frame, however, this is not a fuel tank but a dummy. The fact that it is there just as a piece of trim has enabled Buell to adopt a type of translucent plastic pioneered on the Apple iMac computer. The see-through dummy tank allows the top of the engine to be viewed from above, almost giving the Lightning City XB9SX the air of a working mechanical model rather than a production motorcycle.

The Thunderstorm 984-cc engine, cooled by oil and a powerful, underseat electric fan, hangs low in the frame and the stubby exhaust is mounted not to the side but directly beneath the engine, again to lower the centre of gravity. With its ultra-short wheelbase of 132 cm (52 in.), the Buell lives up to its "Lightning" name in the handling department, and drive is transmitted through a clean and silent belt rather than a conventional chain.

The braking system is unusual, too, in that the front wheel is equipped with a massive, 38.1-cm (15 in.) disc that is bolted to the outer edge of the rim for better distribution of unsprung weight. The wheel is also attached to the inverted Showa racing forks without spacers, nuts or washers, again to save weight.

To complete the urban warrior look, the Lightning City XB9SX is equipped with mesh grilles over the headlights and motocross-style handlebars with deflectors to protect the rider's hands from passing wing mirrors.

CONFEDERATE F113 HELLCAT

As naked motorcycles go, they don't come much more radical than Confederate's new F113 Hellcat. Hand-made and individually designed from the ground up, it is claimed to be the fastest and most luxurious radial-twin American motorcycle ever made.

The result of a fifteen-year design process, the Hellcat is like no other motorcycle you'll ever see. The frame is a unique, patented design and, unlike most small-volume American manufacturers, which use Harley-Davidson engines in their machines, Confederate has built its own powerplant from scratch.

Inspired by the industrial elegance of Bauhaus design, the Hellcat has been purposely left devoid of ornamentation. Every component is there for no other reason than that it plays an essential part in the way the motorcycle goes, stops, and handles.

The New Orleans-based firm has paid an almost obsessive amount of attention to ensuring that there isn't a hint of flex in its motorcycle frames (which, on the Hellcat, incorporate the bike's exhaust system) and that the massive power of the twin-cylinder engine reaches the rear wheel as quickly as possible.

In order to do this, the Hellcat's crankshaft and gearbox output shaft are closer together than on more traditional motorcycles, ensuring the minimum of power loss between engine and final drive.

The result, says Confederate, is "blazing speed and mountains of torque from the smoothest, fastest revving, most durable, best sounding, hardest accelerating American motorcycle ever made".

Some claim indeed, but anyone who has ridden a Confederate agrees that in every respect they are superlative motorcycles. And, unlike most American muscle bikes, the Hellcat even handles well, thanks to being equipped with Penske Racing coil-over shock absorbers, two-piece Lightcon wheels and, perhaps the most conventional components on the whole machine, 50-mm (2 in.) Marzocchi forks.

Engine
1853 cc, air-cooled, single-overhead-camshaft, v-twin
Power
88 kW (118 bhp) @ 6000 rpm (est.)
Torque
183 Nm (135 ft lb) @ 4500 rpm (est.)
Gearbox
Five-speed
Final drive
Chain
Weight
231 kg (510 lb)
Top speed
Not available

DERBI GPR125 NUDE

Engine
124 cc, liquid-cooled, single-cylinder, two-stroke
Power
9 kW (12 bhp) or 16 kW (22 bhp) (est.) @ 8500 rpm
Torque
Not available
Gearbox
Six-speed
Final drive
Chain
Weight
100 kg (220 lb) (est.)
Top speed
80 km/h (50 mph) or 145 km/h (90 mph)

The chance to enjoy "advanced, naked technology", as Derbi describes its new street bike's engineering, need not be confined to riders of large-engined superbikes.

This little Derbi may have only a 125-cc engine but its great looks and state-of-the-art design touches won the Best Open Design award at the 2004 Paris show, where it eclipsed many, much larger contenders.

Based on the company's GPR125 race replica junior sports bike, the Nude lets it all hang out with an exposed engine, a jacked-up rear end and a neat, double-headlight arrangement topped by a small, bubble screen – all essential features for an up-to-the-minute naked bike.

The jewel-like GPR even has a wonderfully delicate exhaust system that snakes up around the engine and over the rear suspension to exit below the aggressively styled tail unit in correct naked fashion.

The v-spoke wheels and beautifully detailed brake discs are also signs that Derbi has left no stone unturned in its quest to build what is effectively a miniature superbike. Even the large, white-faced rev counter with combined digital speedometer wouldn't look out of place on a machine with an engine ten times this size.

But the GPR is not all show and no go. While it will be sold in 9-kW (12 bhp) restricted form in some countries, the engine can put out an estimated 16 kW (22 bhp), making the bike potentially capable of 145 km/h (90 mph).

Combine all this with Derbi's racing success in 2004, when the Spanish firm's works rider Jorge Lorenzo won two Grands Prix and achieved five podium places, and the GPR should prove irresistible to young riders.

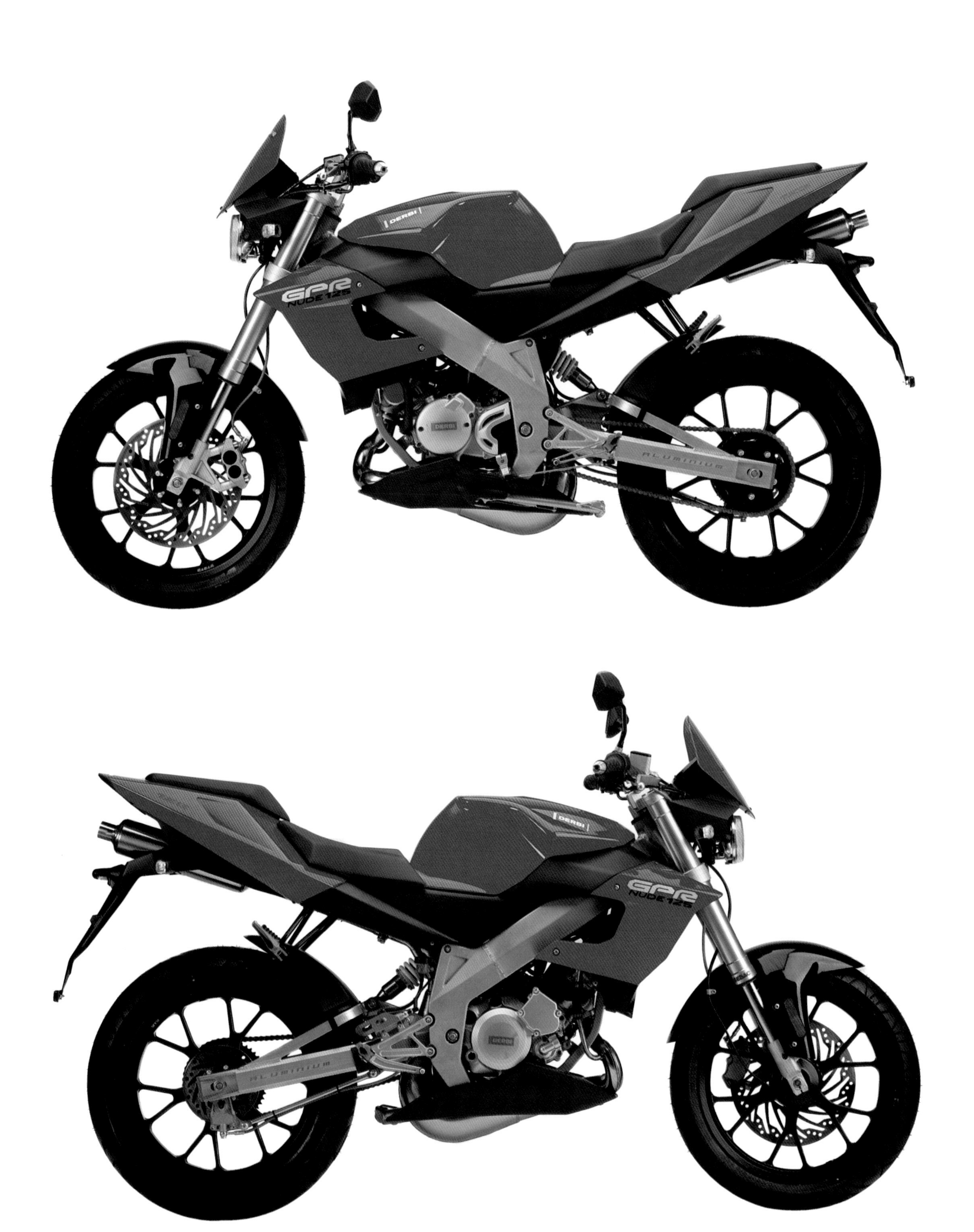
DERBI
GPR
NUDE 125
DERBI
ALUMINIUM
DERBI
GPR
NUDE 125
DERBI
ALUMINIUM

DERBI MULHACÉN/ MULHACÉN CAFÉ

Engine
659 cc, liquid-cooled, single-cylinder, four-valve, four-stroke
Power
36 kW (48 bhp)@ 6000 rpm
Torque
Not available
Gearbox
Five-speed
Final drive
Chain
Weight
160 kg (353 lb)
Top speed
169 km/h (105 mph)

It is not just the Italians who know a thing or two about style. The Spanish clearly do too, for the new Derbi Mulhacén must qualify as one of the neatest-looking middleweight street bikes ever.

Named after a 3500-m (11,480 ft) mountain across which snakes Europe's highest forest track, the Mulhacén is designed for a combination of back-road fun and practical town riding. The pared-down looks are wonderfully cohesive, with a simply beautiful, sweeping fuel tank and seat unit that leads the eye effortlessly from the front to the back of the machine.

The single, high-level exhaust was inspired by the street scrambler bikes of the late 1960s and early 1970s that were popular on America's west coast, but an item such as the Pro Lateral Link monoshock is thoroughly twenty-first-century, with its beefy, aluminium swing arm supporting the back end and giving full exposure to the rear wheel.

Black rims add to the stealthy look, and other modern touches include the 'breaking wave' front brake disc with radial caliper and the elliptical, LCD dashboard.

Derbi is expected to offer a range of mix-and-match accessory options for the Mulhacén, which will allow it to be customized and personalized according to the rider's taste.

A second version, the Mulhacén Café, has also been announced. This will have twin, high-level chrome exhausts exiting on either side of the machine, flat handlebars in the style of the 'Vincent straights' of old, and wire wheels with black, anodized rims.

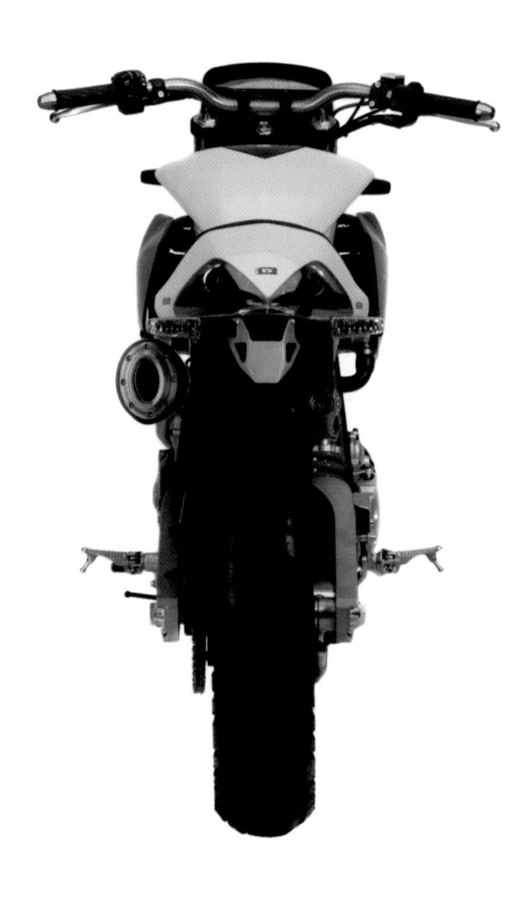

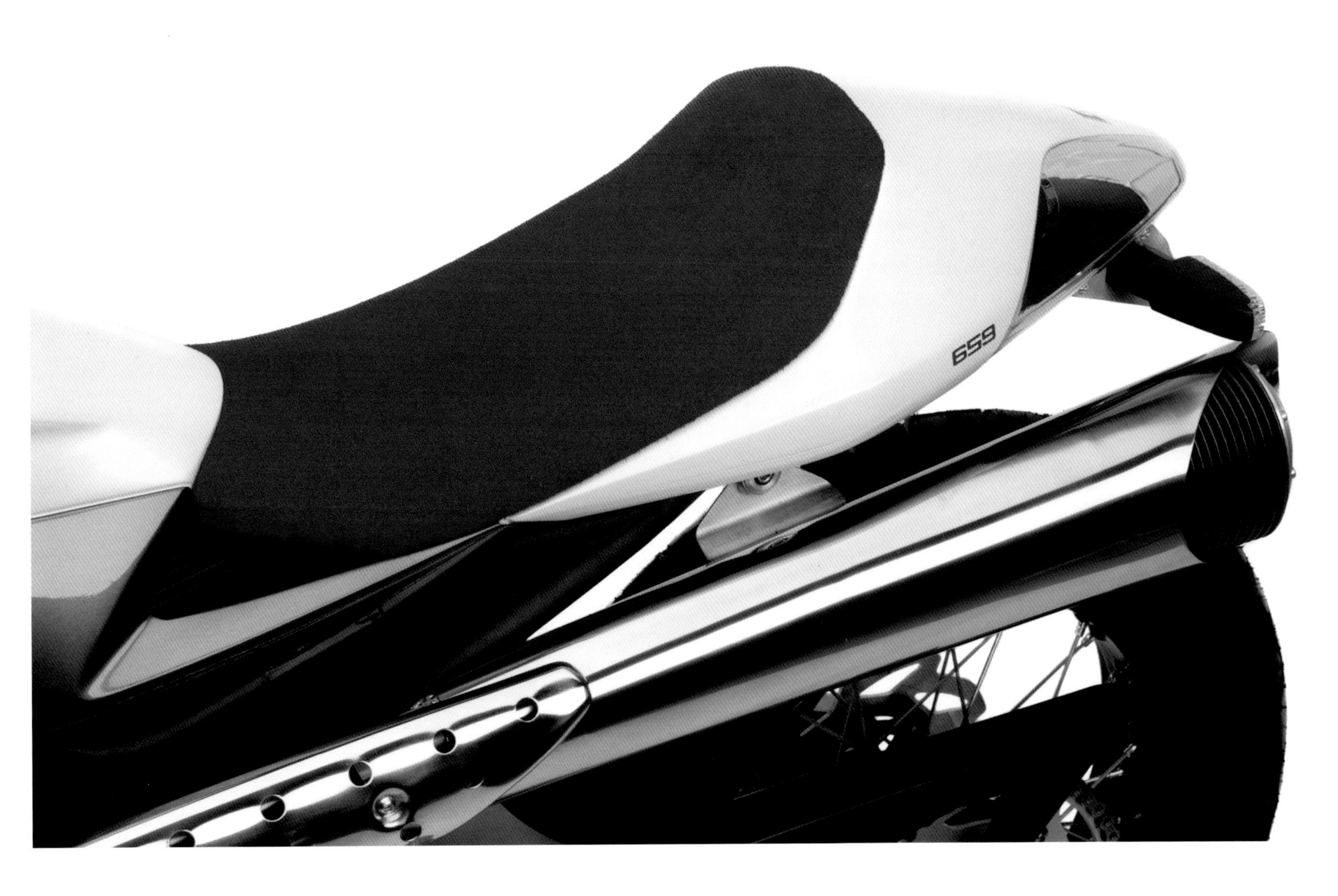
659

DERBI
PRO-LATERAL LINK

DUCATI MULTISTRADA 620 AND 1000S DS

Engine
618 cc (1000S DS 992 cc), air-cooled, fuel-injected, L-twin, two-valve (Desmodromically operated),four-stroke
Power
50 kW (63 bhp) @ 9500 rpm (67 kW/92 bhp @ 7750 rpm)
Torque
56 Nm (41 ft lb) @ 5750 rpm (82 Nm/60 ft lb @ 6750 rpm)
Gearbox
Six-speed
Final drive
Chain
Weight
189 kg (417 lb) (196 kg/432 lb)
Top speed
185 km/h (115 mph) (209 km/h/130 mph)

When the Multistrada was launched in 2003 its claim to fame was that it was the first of a new generation of motorcycles "for all roads". It is an unusual machine, because it looks very like a trail bike yet claims no off-road capability; it is tall, slim and upright yet it handles as well as many a sports bike; it is undoubtedly Ducati in ride and feel, but Ducatis were never meant to be so ugly.

Despite sounding like a mixed-up machine, however, the Multistrada has become one of Ducati's best-selling motorcycles, so it is perhaps no surprise that the Bologna company has decided to offer it with the 620-cc engine from its Monster in a bid to attract new riders.

On reflection, it is the logical thing to do: the Multistrada is a highly capable commuter machine as it is so lithe and nimble, but the standard 1000-cc DS engine – which has the power to make the bike a fine wheelie machine – is rather intimidating for newcomers.

The 620, though, is far less fierce and, of course, cheaper to produce, bringing the mini Multistrada into the same price bracket as much of the less characterful Japanese opposition. For those on a really tight budget, there is even the Multistrada Dark, a matt-black, no-frills offering.

A less sophisticated double-sided swing arm on 620 versions replaces the larger bike's single-sided unit. The 620 bike has a smaller-capacity fuel tank and is lighter overall, although the already tried-and-tested range of Multistrada luggage and performance parts should fit straight on to it.

Once you've served your Multistrada apprenticeship on the 620, it could be time to move up to the latest 1000S DS model, which enhances the standard bike's already fine handling through the use of the Ohlins suspension components found on the 999S sports bike.

Finished in gloss black with the contrasting gold aluminium of the suspension parts, the 1000S DS looks every inch the luxury Multistrada. Its appearance is further embellished by a new handlebar design and the use of carbon fibre for the front mudguard and timing belt cover.

1000S DS
SCORPION

DUCATI

Nowadays the Ducati Monster family might be getting long in the tooth – the original hit the streets more than a decade ago – but it continues to look as fresh as the day it was launched.

Part of the reason for this is that the concept was to design a motorcycle that could be used as a blank canvas for alterations and custom touches that would enhance the iconic shape yet still allow its basic character to show through.

Among the best in-house interpretations of this idea were the S4 and S4R, which use the liquid-cooled engines from the 916 and 996 sports bikes respectively. A less expensive take on the theme is the new S2R, which combines the air-cooled, 803-cc Monster engine with a set of customized-looking, high-level exhausts mounted on the right-hand side, a single-sided swing arm and triple Brembo disc brakes.

The bike also gets Ducati's Adler Power Torque Plate clutch system (APTC), which makes the clutch lighter to use and reduces the risk, ever-present in v-twin bikes, of the rear wheel locking during sharp down changes.

A tiny bikini fairing finishes off the whole job, and five simple but effective paint options make the new Monster stand out from the crowd, helping it look as though it was born yesterday. One of the best of these is a bright tangerine with a black stripe running the length of the bike. The other options are matt black on the budget Dark model, gloss black with a tangerine stripe, Ducati red with a white stripe, and yellow with a black stripe.

It looks like this is one Monster that will never go away.

DUCATI S2R

Engine
803 cc, air-cooled, fuel-injected, l-twin, two-valve (Desmodromically operated), four-stroke

Power
57 kW (77 bhp) @ 8250 rpm

Torque
73 Nm (54 ft lb) @ 6500 rpm

Gearbox
Six-speed

Final drive
Chain

Weight
173 kg (381 lb)

Top speed
209 km/h (130 mph)

HONDA CB 1300 ABS

Engine
1284 cc, liquid-cooled, fuel-injected, double-overhead-camshaft, four-cylinder, four-stroke
Power
85 kW (114 bhp) @ 7500 rpm
Torque
117 Nm (86 ft lb) @ 5500 rpm
Gearbox
Five-speed
Final drive
Chain
Weight
238 kg (525 lb)
Top speed
233 km/h (145 mph)

The CB 1300 'naked' was launched in 2003 to catch the rush of born-again-bikers who were raised on the un-faired 750-cc and 1000-cc Japanese machines of the late 1970s and early 1980s.

This upgraded version retains the requisite retro looks but brings the big CB to a level of engineering refinement that would never have been thought possible twenty-five years ago: not least by the addition of ABS.

The bike's principal feature remains its awesome presence – parked, it looks like an icon of industrial design, that massive engine and huge fuel tank shouting out the message that this is a *real* motorcycle.

Everything on the CB 1300 is big with a capital B. Yet, despite its size, the lines of the muscular Honda flow beautifully: from the mighty, gas-charged rear dampers attached to the beefy swing arm – made from a chunk of 40 mm x 90 mm (1.6 in. x 3.5 in.) box-section alloy – right through to the slightly swept-back handlebars behind the twin electronic dials, and optional cockpit fairing.

By rights, the CB 1300 should be a beast of a bike to handle around town. It never has been, but now it is even smoother and easier to ride at low speeds thanks to the re-mapping of its fuel-injection system. This refreshment of the electronics has also made the most of the large-capacity, four-cylinder engine's greatest asset: its huge mid-range power.

Pumping out 117 Nm (86 ft lb) at 5500 rpm, the CB 1300 manages to match the bike many people regard as the king of torque – Harley-Davidson's Electra Glide – albeit 750 revs higher up the range.

But what this machine is really all about is the reassertion of old-fashioned motorcycling values through state-of-the-art engineering. The CB 1300 is the type of bike that you want throw a pair of saddlebags over, fire up, and see where the road takes you.

Its upright riding position and the absence of substantial fairing preclude prolonged three-figure cruising, but at anywhere between 110 and 145 km/h (68–90 mph) it will lope along comfortably all day, ready and willing to demonstrate the turbine-like thrust of its huge powerplant at the merest tweak of the twist grip.

HONDA

It was Honda that came up with the original concept of putting a mildly detuned sports-bike engine into a tough-looking, 'streetfighter' chassis with sharp handling and eye-popping brakes.

That was in the late 1990s and the machine was evocatively called the Hornet, a name that conjures up just the right combination of aggression, agility, style and punch. The motorcycle became an instant classic, attracting buyers with its combination of then-radical looks and a high level of practicality, thanks to the comfortable, upright riding position and the understressed CB 600 engine.

Not only has the model survived into the twenty-first century but it reaches a wider market than ever, having been joined by a 900-cc big brother that uses a watered-down version of the hugely powerful Fireblade engine.

The latest Hornets have Honda's ultra-rigid 'Mono Backbone' frame, with the 2005 600s being given the first inverted front forks to appear on a naked street bike, sportier instruments and a new air deflector. Apart from that, the model received little more than some new colour schemes to keep it fresh. After all, Hornets already had the underseat exhausts, sturdy lines and punchy engine now considered essential on naked street bikes.

The fact is, however, that machines such as Triumph's Speed Triple and KTM's Super Duke simply go the extra distance in terms of looks, street cred and thrills. In comparison, the Hornet has a rather feeble sting in its tail and can only survive in this form by virtue of its reliability and a loyal fan base.

HONDA HORNET CB 600F/CB 900F

Engine
600 cc (CB900F 919 cc), liquid-cooled, double-overhead-camshaft, in-line four-cylinder, four-stroke
Power
71 kW (95 bhp) @ 12,000 rpm
(80 kW/107 bhp @ 9000 rpm)
Torque
63 Nm (46 ft lb) @ 9500 rpm
(91 Nm/67 ft lb @ 6500 rpm)
Gearbox
Six-speed
Final drive
Chain
Weight
178 kg (392 lb) (194 kg/428 lb)
Top speed
209 km/h (130 mph) (233 km/h/145 mph)

KAWASAKI Z750 S

Engine
748 cc, liquid-cooled, fuel-injected, double-overhead-camshaft, four-cylinder, four-stroke
Power
81 kW (108 bhp) @ 10,500 rpm
Torque
73 Nm (54 ft lb) @ 8000 rpm
Gearbox
Six-speed
Final drive
Chain
Weight
195 kg (430 lb)
Top speed
241 km/h (150 mph)

Kawasaki took an age to replace its reliable yet dull air-cooled, old-fashioned ZR-7 750-cc street bike. But when the new Z750 arrived in 2004 most people agreed it was worth the wait. It had up-to-date looks, a punchy, water-cooled engine taken from a superseded sports bike, sweet handling and a very fair price tag made possible by a no-frills steel frame, basic brakes and suspension and a small, inexpensive bikini fairing.

Thoroughly tried and tested and generally deemed cool, the mid-size Z is now offered with an all-new half fairing that radically alters the character of the bike, turning it from a mean-looking street machine into a rather cosy all-rounder. Ducts in the original's bikini fairing are claimed to have been wind-tunnel-designed to create a protective 'air bubble' effect around the rider. It seems implausible, and it doesn't work.

So, while the half-faired S may not look as business-like as its bikini-clad brother, there is no doubt that it is a much more practical proposition, offering decent weather protection, marginally better performance and economy through improved aerodynamics, and even a little storage space. All this is achieved without sacrificing the Z750's easy handling abilities in town, yet it is now a much more stable and practical motorway tourer.

One of the Z's more interesting design features remains unchanged. In line with the trend for ever-funkier instrumentation, its clock arrangement consists of a dominant, circular, analogue tachometer that has an integrated LCD digital speedometer, all lit up by a deep-red glow.

Kawasaki
Kawasaki

Kawasaki

Kawasaki

KTM SUPER DUKE

Engine
942 cc, liquid-cooled, fuel-injected, 75-degree v-twin, four-stroke
Power
88 kW (118 bhp) @ 8000 rpm
Torque
90 Nm (66 ft lb) @ 7000 rpm
Gearbox
Six-speed
Final drive
Chain
Weight
189 kg (417 lb)
Top speed
241 km/h (150 mph)

For decades the Austrian firm KTM, which was officially established in 1955, made its living building small-engined road bikes and a range of highly competitive off-roaders for a niche market.

The introduction of its supermoto-styled Duke in 1996, however, gave KTM a new lease of life and projected it from being a company known only among the motorcycling cognoscenti to one that was widely regarded as the manufacturer of some of the coolest street bikes around.

Until now KTM has concentrated on off-road or dual-sport bikes, but it has now decided to rattle a few cages in the highly competitive 'naked' market with the introduction of the awesome-looking Super Duke.

Originally shown as a concept bike in 2002, the Super Duke appeared in the real and glorious metal at the 2004 Intermot show. It uses the tried-and-tested 950-cc engine from the Adventure rally bike with a road-based transmission, a unit so tight and compact that it can be contained in a brand-new aluminium frame weighing a mere 10 kg (22 lb).

One of the great strengths of the Super Duke is its handling, which is made ultra-sharp by the bike's short swing arm and very low overall weight: at 189 kg (417 lb), it is claimed to be the lightest twin-cylinder machine in its class.

Unashamedly designed to have fun on, the Super Duke is most at home on fast, twisting back roads where its fine handling and super-torquey v-twin engine can be exploited to the ultimate.

For the first time on a KTM, the Super Duke is fitted with electronic fuel injection with double throttle valves feeding each cylinder for instant response. And, despite having the high standards of finish and build quality for which KTM is famous, the Super Duke is competitively priced when compared with similar machines from Triumph and Ducati.

Let the battle of the streetfighters commence.

MALAGUTI DRAKON

Engine
50 cc, liquid-cooled, single-cylinder, two-stroke
Power
6 kW (8 bhp) (est.)
Torque
Not available
Gearbox
Six-speed
Final drive
Chain
Weight
112 kg (247 lb)
Top speed
56 km/h (35 mph)

Not so long ago any teenager who wanted to ride a motorcycle longed for a scaled-down race replica, but now that nakeds are the in-thing, 'mini-muscle' machines such as Malaguti's purposeful Drakon are set to become all the rage.

It may only have a 50-cc engine, but the little Drakon boasts many a feature found on street bikes twenty times its size: it has an electric starter, LED tail lights, an underseat exhaust with twin catalytic converters and even state-of-the-art radial brakes.

Whereas the 50-cc motorcycles of old made do with a simple, analog speedometer, the Drakon is equipped with a multi-option on-board computer that includes a rev counter, speed, volt meter and clock – it can even tell you your acceleration time from 0–64km/h (0–40 mph).

Weighing just 112 kg (247 lb), the Drakon has such fine handling that it almost seems wasteful that it is available only with such a puny engine. The next step for this seventy-five-year-old firm, still run by the Malaguti family, must surely be to put a version of its 125-cc racing engine into the Drakon's wonderful chassis.

DRAKON

MOTO GUZZI BREVA V1100

Engine
1064 cc, air-cooled, twin-plug, 90-degree v-twin, four-stroke
Power
62 kW (83 bhp) @ 7500 rpm
Torque
87 Nm (64 ft lb) @ 6000 rpm
Gearbox
Six-speed
Final drive
Shaft
Weight
233 kg (514 lb)
Top speed
193 km/h (120 mph)

Moto Guzzi's new Breva represents the civilized face of street biking – it doesn't claim to be a fire-breathing, tarmac-stripping animal of a machine in the manner of the Benelli TNT or Triumph Speed Triple, but a relaxed, unpretentious, naked tourer.

It is the first new-generation Guzzi to be powered by the latest 1064-cc Evolution engine, which produces a modest 62 kW (83 bhp). At first glance the machine may appear to harbour a Guzzi engine of yore but, apart from the distinctive v-twin configuration, the powerplant is completely fresh.

Redesigned con rods and pistons are complemented by twin-plug cylinder heads and an all-new, six speed gearbox to make the Breva entirely twenty-first-century. Moto Guzzi's trademark shaft drive – which is integral to the massive swing arm – has also been upgraded with a new 'reactive' system that is said to eliminate the backlash usually expected with this form of final drive.

A great deal of thought has clearly gone into the creation of this 'quiet man' among street bikes, with endless hours of testing on track and road delaying the launch by almost a year.

But Guzzi wanted the Breva to be a true all-rounder: reliable, responsive, sweet-handling, stable and with a decent turn of speed – and that appears to be what it is.

A significant part of the design brief, however, was to retain the Guzzi character, which means the bike had to have – no offence intended – a slightly agricultural, mechanical feel and not be some whispering, vibration-free zone that insulated itself from the rider.

Despite this, the Italian firm has seen fit to provide the Breva V1100 with a highly advanced 'communicator panel' among the instrument layout. This features an 'active matrix' LCD that can be linked to a series of optional entertainment packages. It also gives fuel consumption, tank range, temperature and trip distance readouts that can be accessed from a hand-grip control while on the move.

To demonstrate the Breva's all-round capability, a set of custom-made luggage has been designed to complement the bike, while other options include ABS and a cruiser-style screen.

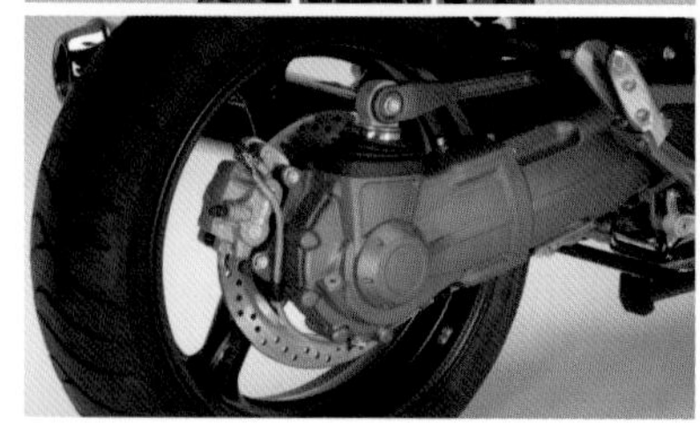

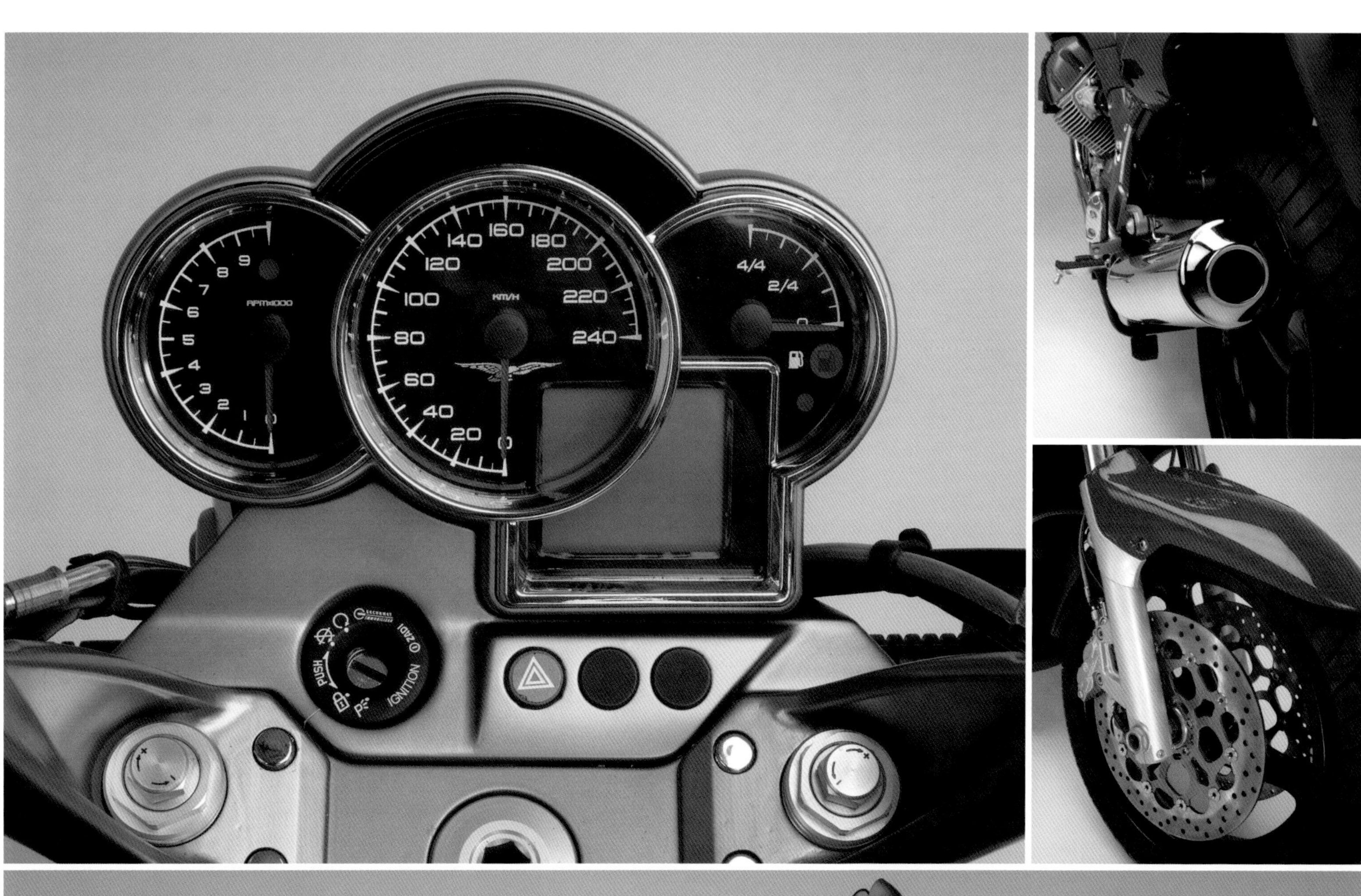
RPMx1000
KM/H
4/4
2/4
PUSH
IGNITION

MOTO GUZZI GRISO

Long, low and lean, the Griso looks like a one-off special from a Californian design studio rather than a full-scale production machine.

Moto Guzzi has been teasing enthusiasts with 'concept' versions of the Griso since 2002 and now it's finally here: an exciting combination of cruiser and naked muscle bike with a touch of touring potential thrown in.

The name "Griso" was inspired by a character in Alessandro Manzoni's novel *I promessi sposi* (*The Betrothed*), which is set near Moto Guzzi's headquarters at Mandello del Lario. Griso was a bodyguard and the bike is supposed to project an image of strength, power and, according to the manufacturer, wickedness.

Among its many interesting design features is the high-level beam frame that sweeps around the fuel tank and down to the massive, single-sided swing arm, which contains the same reactive, anti-backlash shaft drive system used on the firm's Breva.

And, like the Breva, the Griso features a 'siamesed' exhaust system, in which, in the case of this bike, the right-hand pipe wraps around the front of the engine to flow in parallel with its counterpart to a large and rather unattractive silencer. No doubt the designers have already come up with a better-looking alternative.

With hefty 32 cm (12.6 in.) twin disc brakes up front and impressively substantial inverted and fully adjustable forks, the Griso is clearly intended to be a bike that can be ridden hard on the open road. Yet the all-new, 1064 cc 'Evolution' engine that it shares with the Breva has been tuned to provide impressive torque from low revs, to make the bike tractable and easy to handle in traffic.

With its relaxed, upright riding position, separate seats, sensibly located pillion footrests and decent steering lock, the Griso should indeed make for a practical machine on which to do battle in the urban jungle. And with looks like this it will certainly win plenty of street cred.

Engine
1064 cc, air-cooled, twin-plug, 90-degree v-twin, four-stroke
Power
63 kW (85 bhp) @ 7500 rpm
Torque
89 Nm (66 ft lb) @ 6000 rpm
Gearbox
Six-speed
Final drive
Shaft
Weight
225 kg (496 lb)
Top speed
193 km/h (120 mph)

MOTO MORINI CORSARO AND 9½

Originally founded in 1937, Moto Morini survived in the ownership of the same family for fifty years before its name was bought by Cagiva, which let it lie dormant throughout the 1990s.

At the end of the decade, however, Franco Morini bought back the name, vowing to create an entirely new Moto Morini in the spirit of the original machines built by his grandfather.

A business partnership with Gianni Berti, of the Italian washing-machine dynasty, has now made this possible, and at the Bologna Autoshow in December 2004 the Corsaro and 9½ prototypes were unveiled to huge applause.

The reborn firm has taken the difficult route of designing its own engines for the bikes, both of which are liquid-cooled, fuel-injected, v-twin, twin-cam four-strokes designated "Corsa Corto". The engine, created by Franco Lambertini, gives a displacement of 1187 cc for the Corsaro and 998 cc for the 9½, which is named in honour of the legendary Moto Morini 3½, the 350-cc bike of the late 1970s that had an engine also developed by Lambertini.

The Corsaro (Italian for 'pirate') is every inch the modern streetfighter, with minimalist instrumentation, twin headlamps and a swept-back frontal area. Morini designer Luciano Marabese claims the fuel tank and nose fairing are intended to recall "the opening wings of an eagle", and they do, if you use your imagination.

Marabese has made a feature of the hefty plumbing of the underseat exhausts, the downpipes of which curl and snake their way around the bottom of the engine. Mesh air vents in the seat unit and a tiny, faired-in rear light help to complete a minimalist, no-nonsense image.

Sturdy Marzocchi superbike forks support the front end, while the steel trellis frame appears to have been inspired by Ducati but is no less a thing of beauty for it.

While the Corsaro is intended to be an uncompromising, high-performance street bike – its claimed 104 kW (140 bhp) puts it among the most powerful machines in its class – the less expensive 9½ is a milder creature altogether and designed for greater versatility.

It has something of a retro feel with wire-spoked, rather than cast, wheels, a less substantial swing arm and a two-into-one, high-level exhaust system reminiscent of those used on street scrambler bikes in the 1970s.

Although softer than the Corsaro's, the 9½'s engine still punches out 78 kW (105 bhp). Since it is simply a smaller capacity version of the Corsaro unit, however, it is sturdy and free-revving.

Engine
1187 cc (9½ 998 cc) liquid-cooled, fuel-injected, 87-degree v-twin, four-stroke
Power
104 kW (140 bhp) @ 8500 rpm (78 kW/105 bhp @ 9000 rpm)
Torque
123 Nm (91 ft lb) @ 6500 rpm (102 Nm/75 ft lb @ 7000 rpm)
Gearbox
Six-speed
Final drive
Chain
Weight
198 kg (437 lb) (180 kg/397 lb est.)
Top speed
241 km/h (150 mph) (217 km/h/135 mph)

MV AGUSTA BRUTALE

Engine
749 cc, liquid-cooled, double-overhead-camshaft, four-cylinder, four-stroke
Power
95 kW (127 bhp) @ 12,500 rpm
Torque
69 Nm (51 ft lb) @ 9000 rpm
Gearbox
Six-speed cassette unit
Final drive
Chain
Weight
179 kg (395 lb)
Top speed
241 km/h (150 mph)

The manufacturers of naked street bikes unashamedly sell them on the basis that they look mean, menacing and, well, brutal; yet MV Agusta's Brutale somehow contrives to be beautiful too.

First launched in 2001, the Brutale arrived on the scene at the vanguard of the current trend for nakeds, which made its peculiar, pancake-shaped headlamp and attacking stance seem all the more remarkable.

Primarily created to make the most of the financial and technological investment that went into developing the 750-cc F4 sports bike, the Brutale now sits slightly uneasily among its rivals for two reasons: first, until the recent introduction of a 1000 cc version, it was one of the smallest-capacity machines in its class and secondly, along with the Kawasaki Z1000, it is the only one to have a four-cylinder engine.

This is significant, because the low-down torque and instant take-off provided by the opposition's v-twin and 'triple' engines are intrinsic to the character of the modern naked. In contrast, the MV's revvy four-cylinder unit must be worked hard and kept on the boil in order to maintain progress. This can be a nuisance when battling through city traffic but, as with a thoroughbred racehorse, a masterful hand makes for an exhilarating ride.

Perhaps, then, the Brutale is 'the thinking man's naked' or maybe even 'the rich man's naked'. It is considerably more expensive than the competition, but that is only to be expected of a machine sporting the MV badge. Naturally, fine handling has been made a priority and in this department the Brutale is possibly a class leader. The finish and quality of this bike's components are also superb, from the neat, twin-stack exhaust pipes (which produce one of the most heavenly sounds in motorcycling) to the inverted Marzocchi racing forks and the six-piston brake calipers. Carbon fibre surrounds the digital instrument console and the way the fuel tank flows into the seat and tail unit is simply a work of art.

A beautiful brute indeed.

BRUTALE
CRC
AGUSTA
BRUTALE
CRC
AGUSTA

MZ 1000SF

Engine
998 cc, liquid-cooled, double-overhead-camshaft, parallel-twin, four-stroke
Power
87 kW (117 bhp) @ 9000 rpm
Torque
95 Nm (70 ft lb) @ 7000 rpm
Gearbox
Six-speed
Final drive
Chain
Weight
200 kg (441 lb)
Top speed
217 km/h (135 mph)

Not long after surprising the world with the performance and capabilities of its new 1000S sports tourer, MZ, a marque once known only for building smoke-belching, utilitarian two-strokes, is attacking the street-bike market with the meaty-looking 1000SF.

Entirely based on the S, it has been given the street look by the simple expedients of replacing the full fairing with an aerodynamic nose cowl, raising the handlebars, adding a close-fitting bellypan and offering some colour schemes that are less subtle than the soft silver or black of its sibling. The new bike also comes with a quickly detachable rear-seat cowling that has a low-rise backstop to give comfortable solo cruising.

Slightly altered fuel and ignition mapping ensures the SF gets plenty of mid-range power – essential for a successful street bike.

For the reborn MZ to be a success, however, might take more than the SF can offer. Despite the quality finish, good performance, sound handling and (to date) reliability, this machine is not scaring the opposition in the way that MZ would have liked.

Relatively few have sold in Europe since its launch, and many people believe the German-based firm has bitten off more than it can chew by entering the ultra-competitive 1-litre market so soon after being bought by the far-eastern Hong Leong Industries group.

It is widely thought that MZ might be better off building on that utilitarian heritage by concentrating on the smaller, Yamaha-engined commuter bikes it makes alongside its 1000-cc machines.

SHARK

SUZUKI GSF650

Suzuki's Bandit 600 has been one of the great success stories of modern motorcycle design, selling tens of thousands of units since it was launched in 1993. The conventional but pleasing shape and specification made it all things to all men (and women, thanks to its easy handling) and Bandits the world over have been used as racers, commuters, courier bikes and often as the basis for radical custom machines.

Its many fans were understandably concerned, therefore, to learn that the model was in for a makeover that has endowed it with a bigger engine and some significant alterations to its appearance.

The overbored engine features new, domed pistons and is claimed to deliver greater low- and mid-range torque with smoother power throughout the rev range, better throttle response and harder acceleration.

A new, lightweight, stainless-steel exhaust system is a practical but unusually extravagant touch to find on a relatively inexpensive motorcycle. The seat height is adjustable by up to 20 mm (0.8 in.) and the handlebars by up to 10 mm (0.4 in.). The distinctive Bandit fuel tank has been replaced by a shorter but deeper unit that holds the same amount of fuel lower down in the frame, so lowering the machine's centre of gravity.

Sadly, the honest nature of the original Bandit is betrayed by some rather cheap-looking plastic panels intended to trim the frame near the front of the fuel tank.

The Bandit 600 is available in traditional 'naked' form or as an S variant with a reasonably attractive and quite effective half fairing.

Engine
656 cc, air-cooled, double-overhead-camshaft, four-cylinder, four-stroke
Power
60 kW (80 bhp) @ 10,500 rpm
Torque
61 Nm (45 ft lb) @ 9500 rpm
Gearbox
Six-speed
Final drive
Chain
Weight
201 kg (443 lb)
Top speed
193 km/h (120 mph)

SUZUKI SV650/SV1000

Lots of newly qualified riders long to own a Ducati, but often they have fears – usually unfounded nowadays – of endless breakdowns and poor durability.

These are the people who might buy Suzuki's SV650, a Japanese alternative to the Ducati Monster with proven reliability from a bullet-proof engine, sharp handling and looks that have clearly been created by a Japanese computer rather than the pen of a passionate Italian designer.

Nevertheless, the SV650 has been hugely popular since its launch, and the latest K5 model has sharper styling that echoes the v-twin engine configuration. Available as a naked or a half-faired 'S' version with a sportier riding position, the SV650 provides the perfect introduction to the delights of v-twin motorcycling.

Despite its mid-sized engine, it still develops the kind of low-range power that riders of high-revving, four-cylinder machines can only dream about. The SV punches out of corners hard, giving the impression of a much more powerful machine than it is, and offers a useful level of engine braking that makes bend-swinging a delight.

The new SV1000 K4 provides more of the same with considerably greater engine power and is intended to be the natural progression from the 650 for riders who have cut their teeth on the smaller machine and now want a bike that offers greater distance capability and sharper performance.

Engine
645 cc (SV1000 996 cc), liquid-cooled, double-overhead-camshaft, v-twin, four-stroke
Power
54 kW (72 bhp) @ 9000 rpm
(89 kW/120 bhp @ 9000 rpm)
Torque
64 Nm (47 ft lb)@ 7200 rpm
(102 Nm/75 ft lb @ 7200 rpm)
Gearbox
Six-speed
Final drive
Chain
Weight
165 kg (364 lb) (187 kg/412 lb)
Top speed
209 km/h (130mph) (233 km/h /145 mph)

TRIUMPH SPEED TRIPLE

Engine
1050 cc, fuel-injected, double-overhead-camshaft, three-cylinder, four-stroke
Power
97 kW (130 bhp) @ 9100 rpm
Torque
105 Nm (77 ft lb) @ 5100 rpm
Gearbox
Six-speed
Final drive
Chain
Weight
189 kg (417 lb)
Top speed
241 km/h (150 mph)

There's only one way to describe Triumph's new street bike. It's an exercise in naked aggression. This is the motorcycle that every custom 'streetfighter' builder of the past decade has probably been trying to create.

With its high-level, tucked-in exhausts, its twin, bug-eyed headlights and its squat, attacking riding position, it seems that the Speed Triple's designers have left no room for improvement through the addition of after-market parts.

But the best thing about this bike – if anything could be better than those wild looks – is that it isn't all mouth and no trousers. For this it has to thank an all-new, 1050-cc, long-stroke engine that punches out 97 kW (130 bhp) and is described by Triumph as the machine's "primal three-cylinder core".

The wheelbase has been shortened by 11 mm (½ in.) over the original Speed Triple, while the old model's good handling has been outclassed through the addition of Showa inverted racing forks, a new aluminium frame and a redesigned, single-sided swing arm.

Huge, 32-cm (12½ in.) twin disc brakes with radial calipers apply 'giant hand' stopping power to the front, while the overall aesthetic is enhanced by trendy touches such as an LED rear light, clear-lens indicators and an apparent lack of engine hoses. They are there – it's just that Triumph's designers have managed to hide them all away to obtain a clean, mean look.

Apart from the rather thin and ungenerous seat, the Speed Triple is a machine far more practical as an all-rounder than its looks should allow. The short wheelbase, low seat height and torquey engine make it ideal for town work; it has enough power to eat up the open road, and its combination of speed and handling should make it a joy on the track. And, of course, it produces that distinctive, three-cylinder sound that can be enhanced with a set of Triumph's free-flowing exhausts.

This is a motorcycle that will leave the world's most talented designers of hand-built custom specials crying into their beer.

15:26
TRIUMPH
MIN x 1000

SPEED TRIPLE

Fazer

Arai

YAMAHA FZ6S, FZ6 FAZER, FZS1000S FAZER, FZS1000 FAZER

Yamaha's Fazer range has always been a direct rival to Honda's Hornet, but the manufacturer's new-generation middleweights leave that particular member of the opposition for dead.

The most popular model is sure to be the unfaired FZ6S, which uses a retuned engine from the R6 sports bike suspended from the high-tech, ultra-light, ultra-rigid, die-cast-aluminium Yamaha CF frame.

The FZ6S and the half-faired FZ6 Fazer, both of which have 600-cc engines, are the first Yamaha street machines to be given this exotic chassis, which until now has been used only on the company's more expensive sports bikes. It is made from two separate sections that are glued together using aviation-type engineering.

Not only does the CF frame give the two 600-cc FZ machines an appearance that is totally up to date, it also endows them with the type of handling that makes riders of pure sports machines wonder why they spent the extra money.

Light, agile and with plenty of power – spoilt only by a 'hole' in the mid range that calls for lots of gear changing and revving to keep the engine in the powerband – the naked FZ6S in particular is made for pure fun.

On this bike, the highly sculpted fuel tank gives way to a set of wide handlebars and then, from the rider's perspective, apparently nothing else. This is due to the slimness of the unusually shaped, multi-faceted headlamp, which is claimed to be an aerodynamic aid.

At the other end of the bike, the passenger section of the seat rises above the rider's cut-down section, resulting in extra comfort for the passenger and a feeling of being 'in' rather than 'on' the bike for the rider.

Yamaha offers the option of a larger-engined bike in the form of the FZS1000S Fazer and the FZS1000 Fazer. Both of these machines are faired and are powered by a version of the R1 sports-bike engine on a conventional, tubular chassis.

Engine
600 cc (FZ1000S Fazer and FZS1000 Fazer 998 cc), double-overhead-camshaft, four-cylinder, four-stroke
Power
73 kW (98 bhp) @ 12,000 rpm (107 kW/143 bhp @ 10,000 rpm)
Torque
63 Nm (46 ft lb) @ 10,000 rpm (106 Nm/78 ft lb @ 7500 rpm)
Gearbox
Six-speed
Final drive
Chain
Weight
187 kg (412 lb) (208 kg/459 lb)
Top speed
225 km/h (140 mph) (249 km/h/155 mph)

YAMAHA MT-01

Engine
1670 cc, air-cooled, fuel-injected, double-overhead-camshaft, v-twin, four-stroke
Power
67 kW (90 bhp) @ 4750 rpm
Torque
150 Nm (111 ft lb) @ 3750 rpm
Gearbox
Five-speed
Final drive
Chain
Weight
240 kg (529 lb)
Top speed
217 km/h (135 mph) (est.)

For most visitors to the 2004 Intermot show the Yamaha MT-01 was the bike of the moment: almost 1700 cc of the beefiest-looking street machine ever to roll off a Japanese production line.

But a motorcycle like this, which follows in the hallowed path of Yamaha's legendary V-Max street bike, could never be allowed to leave the manufacturer's drawing board without being on the far side of radical – and that's exactly what the MT-01 is.

The massive, 1670-cc v-twin powerplant is derived from Yamaha's Road Star cruiser but is retuned to produce 67 kW (90 bhp) and drives through a chain rather than a power-sapping shaft. The engine dominates the machine, hanging down low from the stubby chassis to give what the manufacturer describes as "sports handling" characteristics.

Although far from lithe at a claimed 240 kg (529 lb), the MT-01 has a massive torque output that makes for rocket-like pull and thrilling roll-on acceleration, even if the riding position, weight and lack of a fairing restrict outright speed to a relatively lowly 217 km/h (135 mph).

The thinking behind the MT-01 is that it should provide a raw motorcycling experience, so Yamaha has deliberately allowed the character of the engine to show so that the rider "feels every piston stroke" through a "pulsating, soul-grabbing, Kodo beat", Kodo being a Japanese musical rhythm.

The titanium exhausts have even been designed to be heard clearly from the seat of the bike without causing a noise nuisance beyond it. Even so, in anticipation of the demand from owners to make their MT-01s as rorty as possible, Yamaha is offering three different tuning kits with track-only exhaust systems.

There seems little doubt that the MT-01 will attract a cult following not unlike that of the V-Max, which was a consistently good seller for around fifteen years.

AKRAPOVIC
MT-01

ADVENTURE SPORTS

APRILIA CAPONORD AND CAPONORD RALLY RAID

Engine
998 cc, liquid-cooled, fuel-injected, twin-plug, 60-degree v-twin, four-valve, four-stroke
Power
73 kW (98 bhp) @ 8250 rpm
Torque
97 Nm (71 ft lb) @ 6250 rpm
Gearbox
Six-speed
Final drive
Chain
Weight
215 kg (474 lb)
Top speed
209 km/h (130 mph)

As an alternative to the Japanese v-twin adventure sports machines, Aprilia's Caponord represents a tempting proposition. With an engine derived from the RSV Mille sports bike and suitably softened for touring and off-road work, the Caponord packs plenty of punch on the open road. It may not match the KTM 950 Adventure for off-road capability, but it far outstrips the Oriental opposition.

Proof that Aprilia intends the Caponord to be taken as seriously as the KTM and BMW GS Adventure in the globetrotting stakes is found in the Rally Raid version, aimed at the hard-core tourist in search of uncharted lands. This is the only machine in its class to be sold complete with aluminium panniers as standard plus two pairs of tyres – one pair for road and light trail use, the other for seriously getting to grips with remote, unsurfaced byways.

Unlike the many manufacturers who are apologetic about the lofty dimensions of their bikes in this category, Aprilia says that the fact that the Rally Raid's seat is 86 cm (33.9 in.) off the ground makes it easier to ride while standing on the footrests. Such a position is standard practice on rough, loose surfaces as it makes the motorcycle feel lighter and therefore easier to control.

The seat is narrow, to ease back and forth movement for quicker weight distribution, and the rubber footrest sleeves can be removed to reveal serrated metal pegs that give maximum grip for boots in muddy conditions.

Rally-derived features abound, such as competition-quality, tapered handlebars with brush guards, a new front mudguard designed for minimal clogging, a nitrogen-filled monoshock, race-quality Brembo brakes, a carbon-fibre engine guard and an aluminium bash plate.

The aluminium-magnesium frame is a class-leader, while the stainless-steel exhaust system should last the life of the bike. A new, slimmer and less cumbersome cockpit fairing contains a comprehensive instrument set-up of clock, ambient temperature thermometer, coolant and fuel gauges and twin trip meters.

The backlighting is adjustable to three different levels and there are warning lights for system malfunction and service intervals, as well as a 12-volt power socket capable of operating items such as a tyre pump, water heater or thermal clothing.

Fully equipped, the Rally Raid offers an impressive carrying capacity: each pannier holds 40 litres (1.4 cu. ft), an optional top box can accommodate a further 50 litres (1.75 cu. ft) and a 23-litre (0.8 cu. ft) tank bag is available. The passenger section of the seat can be removed to provide an extra carrying platform, and Aprilia claims that the 215 kg (474 lb) machine is capable of safely supporting a rider, passenger and luggage weighing together more than 200 kg (441 lb).

aprilia
Caponord

aprilia
Tibet
Raid

aprilia

APRILIA PEGASO AND PEGASO TUSCANY TIBET RAID

Big, 1-litre adventure bikes are great for their high-speed capability, endless pulling power and huge carrying capacity – but drop one out in the desert and getting it upright again is a major logistical problem.

This is where lightweight, single-cylinder dual-purpose machines such as the Pegaso come into their own. They are comfortable cruising the highway at around 121 km/h (75 mph), but when the time comes to turn off the beaten track they can keep up – and often outpace – machines of twice their size. Their nimbleness helps them skip over obstacles, sprint up slippery slopes and glide across loose surfaces.

The standard Pegaso uses a Yamaha engine that is the most sophisticated in its class. This liquid-cooled single-cylinder powerplant with electronic fuel injection, a double overhead camshaft and five valves makes for a flexible in-town commuter machine that will both hold its own on the motorway and make light work of off-road riding.

Like its bigger brother, the Caponord, the Pegaso is also offered in a version fully kitted out for adventure. This bike, the Tuscany Tibet Rally Raid, certainly has proved its worth: two were used to traverse the highest road in the world. The model was chosen to deliver charitable donations to the Leh children's village in Tibet, reachable on a motorcycle only via an unmetalled route 5680 metres (18,635 ft) above sea level.

Standard Tuscany Tibet Rally Raids come complete with a copious aluminium top box, 25 mm (1 in.) more suspension travel than ordinary models, off-road tyres and a cross-braced handlebar designed to accept bolt-on accessories such as compasses and road books.

The machine's 21-litre (4.6 gallons) fuel tank gives a range of up to 402 km (250 miles) between fill-ups, and optional extras include a larger top box with a capacity of 50 litres (1.75 cu. ft), 40-litre (1.4 cu. ft) twin panniers and a centre stand to ease wheel changing in the wilds.

Engine
651 cc, liquid-cooled, fuel-injected, double-overhead-camshaft, single-cylinder, five-valve, four-stroke

Power
37 kW (50 bhp) @ 6250 rpm

Torque
61 Nm (45 ft lb) @ 5200 rpm

Gearbox
Five-speed

Final drive
Chain

Weight
168 kg (370 lb)

Top speed
161 km/h (100 mph)

APRILIA PEGASO STRADA

Engine
659 cc, liquid-cooled, double-overhead-camshaft, single-cylinder, five-valve, four-stroke
Power
36 kW (48 bhp) @ 6000 rpm
Torque
58.4 Nm (43 ft lb) @ 5250 rpm
Gearbox
Five-speed
Final drive
Chain
Weight
168 kg (370 lb)
Top speed
169 km/h (105 mph)

Aprilia's new take on the roadable supermoto theme is based on the now discontinued Pegaso trail/adventure sports machine.

Powered by the liquid-cooled, single-cylinder engine used in Yamaha's XT660, the Pegaso Strada delivers far less focused performance than the more single-minded supermoto models from manufacturers such as KTM and Husqvarna.

This is deliberate, because the bike is intended to project a rough, tough image while avoiding the raw features of the full-blown supermoto, notably an unforgiving suspension, a harsh ride and a peaky engine. As Aprilia puts it: "Going to work can be fun!"

Up-to-date graphics, a neat, eye-catching nose fairing and a very purposeful stance give the Strada a character all of its own. To complete the supermoto look, the bike has a lovely set of blue cast-alloy wheels from Aprilia's RSV-R Mille super-sports machine that are clad in fat, grippy tyres. And look at those turn signals, which must be the smallest fitted to any production motorcycle.

The Strada has been given a generous amount of steering lock to make it ultra-manoeuvrable in tight urban situations and the front forks and rear monoshock are multi-adjustable for pillion carrying or coping with variable surface conditions.

Up front, a huge disc gripped by a Brembo racing-brake caliper provides sufficient stopping power to stand the bike on its nose.

One of the Strada's neatest features, however, is a small button on the handlebars. Press this and the centre of the dummy fuel tank flips up to reveal a useful storage bay with room for a mobile telephone, maps, wallet and so on.

A comprehensive range of accessories was also developed along with the bike, including hand guards, taller screens, heated grips and alternative seats and footrests. ABS is also an option.

BMW F650 GS/ F650 GS DAKAR

Engine
652 cc, water-cooled, four-valve, double-overhead-camshaft, twin-spark, single-cylinder, four stroke
Power
37 kW (50 bhp) @ 6500 rpm
Torque
60Nm (44 ft lb) @ 4800 rpm
Gearbox
Five-speed
Final drive
Chain
Weight
175.4 kg (386 lb)
Top speed
169 km/h (105 mph)

The F650 GS may be BMW's entry level machine, but in its class it is one of the most capable motorcycles on the market. Tried, tested and developed in the gruelling conditions of the Paris–Dakar rally, the baby GS combines roadable refinement with proven competition genes.

The BMW Paris–Dakar race bikes may not look much like the production offering, but beneath the disguise of their ultra-long range fuel tanks and massive suspension travel lurks the GS you can buy in the showrooms – albeit with an engine tuned to the max.

The basic F650 is intended to be a flexible commuter machine with gentle off-road ability. Its generous turning circle and trim dimensions make it ideal for cutting through queues of traffic and it is easy to park in the crowded city. The new, liquid-cooled single-cylinder engine, meanwhile, packs enough punch for occasional motorway work.

On this latest model, extra thought has been given to protecting the rider from the elements with a more efficient fairing with a windscreen which can be quickly removed to make the bike more suitable for off-road use.

Popular with women riders, the GS now has a reduced clutch span which is easier for those with a small hand span to operate and the bike can be supplied with a 30 mm lower seat height (780 mm is standard) – or, for taller riders, a 40 mm higher one.

Additional features include an on-board power socket which allows the battery to be recharged while still on the machine. A jump-start point also enables safe starting from another vehicle in the event of a flat battery – a useful touch on a big single cylinder machine with no kickstarter.

The sturdy luggage rack is designed to accommodate BMW's own overlanding luggage and has strong lassing points built-in.

The Dakar version, meanwhile "differs only in those areas that become vital when negotiating severe terrain, hostile environments and climatic extremes", according to BMW.

This means it gets a larger front wheel – 21 in. instead of 19 in. – an extended front mudguard, hand protectors, 210 mm of suspension travel (40 mm more than standard) and pukka enduro racing tyres. It is also marked out by its single, distinctive colour scheme of pearl white and blue.

24
DAKAR
F650GS

Arai
AFRICAN
ADVENTURE

BMW R1150 GS ADVENTURE

Along with KTM's 950 Adventure, BMW's R1150 GS Adventure is possibly the ultimate in off-the-shelf, hard-core, two-wheeled, all-terrain tourers. To call it motorcycling's equivalent of a Range Rover does not do it justice, as it can reach places that people in four-wheel-drives can only dream of getting to.

It can be supplied with a full overlanding pack, which includes a 30-litre (6.6 gallons) fuel tank, permitting a range of more than 480 km (300 miles), special lug tyres for tackling sand and mud, and a cleverly designed aluminium luggage system.

The side panniers, which contain waterproof holdalls, lock to folding pannier racks and can easily be removed to prevent theft or to allow the racks to carry extra fuel or water containers. Both the racks and the matching rear box have tying points for attaching additional equipment, such as a tent.

Three electrical sockets provide power for heated clothing, a map-reading light and a shock-resistant satellite navigation system accurate to within 10 m (33 ft), this last an optional extra.

An ultra-low first gear lets the bike chug along at just 3–5 km/h (2–3 mph), making it possible to tackle steep, winding ascents on loose surfaces without using large throttle openings that could cause rear-wheel spin. On good roads the 1150-cc engine provides comfortable all-day cruising at 129 km/h (80 mph) in top gear, with fuel consumption of about 17.9 kmpl (50 mpg).

Since this bike is expected to be used in remote areas, the fuel system can be adjusted by fitting an alternative plug into the engine management system that allows the engine to run on low-grade fuel. And, despite BMW's reputation for reliability, the Adventure comes with a minimalist tool kit designed to fit almost every nut and bolt on the machine.

A dirt-repellent, easy-clean black finish is available for the crankcases and wheel rims.

Engine
1130 cc, air- and oil- cooled, single-overhead-camshaft, l-twin, four-valve, four-stroke

Power
71 kW (95 bhp) @ 6750 rpm

Torque
98 Nm (72 ft lb) @ 5250 rpm

Gearbox
Six-speed

Final drive
Shaft

Weight
253 kg (558 lb)

Top speed
193 km/h (120 mph)

BMW R1200 GS

Engine
1170 cc, air- and oil-cooled, single-overhead-camshaft, l-twin, four-valve, four-stroke
Power
75 kW (100 bhp) @ 7100 rpm
Torque
115 Nm (85 ft lb) @ 6200 rpm
Gearbox
Six-speed
Final drive
Shaft
Weight
199 kg (439 lb)
Top speed
48 km/h (30 mph)

BMW launched its first production, dual-purpose bike more than twenty-five years ago. The 800-cc R80 GS developed a huge, worldwide following and the original concept gradually developed into a highly sophisticated machine that was as good for motorway cruising as it was for discovering remote dirt tracks.

By 1999 cylinder capacity had grown to 1150 cc and it was apparent that the GS was being used more on the road than off it, with owners finding its high, comfortable riding position, torquey, air-cooled, flat-twin engine, and compliant suspension ideal for all types of work.

And so it is that the latest GS, enlarged to 1200 cc, is marginally more road-orientated than previous models. It appears in the showroom on road tyres, anti-lock brakes and cast-alloy wheels are standard options, and all models are fitted with a transponder immobilizer.

The distinctive fairing and height-adjustable screen, integrated with the secondary, high-level mudguard, have been styled to give the GS a highly characteristic 'face' and are part of what BMW's aesthetics team refer to as the 'body' of the machine.

Surfaces of this 'body' are finished in plastic, paint or aluminium, depending on their function, and twelve different colour combinations are achievable from three basic colours, two seat colours and two further colours for the fuel tank's side covers.

The tank, which has a capacity of 20 litres (4.4 gallons), is made from impact-proof plastic and has a slender rear portion designed to give leg and knee support during off-road riding.

The seat is ergonomically designed, using a formula based on the rider's step length, to ensure that shorter owners will be able to establish ground contact despite the bike's large dimensions. A plastic cover beneath the removable passenger portion of the seat serves as an extension of the luggage platform.

In true BMW tradition, an extensive range of custom-made luggage has been designed to enhance the GS's abilities as a superb long-distance machine capable of tackling both the smoothest road and the most rutted track. An extensive list of optional extras is available, including electrically heated handlebar grips, seats lower or higher than the standard height, hoops to protect the protruding engine cylinders and a satellite navigation system.

HONDA TRANSALP

Engine
647 cc, liquid-cooled, single-overhead-camshaft, v-twin, four-stroke
Power
39 kW (52 bhp) @ 7500 rpm
Torque
55 Nm (41 ft lb) @ 5500 rpm
Gearbox
Five-speed
Final drive
Chain
Weight
191 kg (421 lb)
Top speed
177 km/h (110 mph)

Honda's Transalp was the bike that started the craze of adventure sports way back in 1987: a brilliant combination of the tried-and-tested v-twin engine from the NTV650 road bike (known for its amazing longevity) and a large, comfortable, trail-bike chassis.

A Transalp will take you to work and provide a fun Sunday afternoon trail riding or bend swinging on a rural back road. A Transalp will take you for a weekend away, a fortnight's holiday or a year-long trip around the world – it's that versatile.

No wonder, then, that Honda has found it hard to improve on such a winning formula. The latest Transalp, now with a 647-cc engine, is Honda's only mid-range, adventure sports option following the discontinuation of the 750-cc Africa Twin, the next step up being the 1000-cc Varadero.

The new model does get a few tweaks in the styling department to keep it up to date, however. Examples of this attention are its black-finished and therefore more practical wheel rims, contemporary clear indicator lenses, a tinted screen, fresh graphics and a redesigned Transalp tank logo. The tips of its practical, stainless-steel exhausts have also been altered to give it a lighter, more pared-down look.

Apart from that, the bike is just as it always was – and just how an adventure sports machine should be – with its high, wide handlebars for manoeuvrability on and off road, a seat comfortable enough for two, a long-range fuel tank for 322-km (200-mile) stints, and, at the heart of it all, that understressed engine.

A hefty bash plate protects the sump and crankcase from rock damage during those occasional off-road forays and triple disc brakes provide all the stopping power needed to comfortably slow down a fully laden Transalp from the type of motorway cruising speeds made possible by the small but effective fairing.

HONDA
HONDA

HONDA

HONDA VARADERO

Engine
996 cc, liquid-cooled, fuel-injected, double-overhead-camshaft, 90-degree v-twin, eight-valve
Power
69 kW (93 bhp) @ 8000 rpm
Torque
88 Nm (65 ft lb) @ 6000 rpm
Gearbox
Six-speed
Final drive
Chain
Weight
253 kg (558 lb)
Top speed
209 km/h (130 mph)

Apart from the fact that the Varadero has liquid cooling, there is little to choose between this machine, Suzuki's V-Strom, and Kawasaki's KLV 1000, but it is the Honda name that makes it the most popular of the bunch by far. The company started the trend for Japanese, one-litre, v-twin adventure sports machines and, as we all know, imitation is the sincerest form of flattery.

The Varadero, named after a Cuban coastal town, offers a more comprehensive specification than its direct competitors, having what amounts to a 'full fairing' thanks to a deeply sculpted fuel tank that allows the rider's legs to be tucked well in from the wind stream. The upper screen and cockpit area flows down into a bellypan that provides protection for the engine and exhaust downpipes.

In common with its rivals, the bike has simple, three-spoke cast wheels that make for easy cleaning. These, however, betray the Varadero's road bias, for a true off-road machine would usually be equipped with spoked rims, which are less vulnerable to terminal damage on poor surfaces.

The two-part seat is among the most comfortable in its class, keeping rider and passenger separate and offering additional space for carrying luggage when the machine is ridden solo.

Criticized in the past for having brakes that failed to live up to its 209-km/h (130 mph) performance, the Varadero now gets an efficient ABS system. Although it is switchable, this addition further confirms that the machine is intended primarily for the road.

Despite its limited off-road credentials, however, the Varadero calls into question the relevance of the traditional long-distance touring bike. If a machine such as this can cruise all day at three-figure speeds, travel hundreds of miles between fuel stops, carry two people and their luggage in comfort *and* take happily to an unmetalled track, why would anyone choose a less versatile 'ordinary' tourer?

VARADERO
HONDA

VARADERO
HONDA

0
20
40
60
80
100
120
140
160
180
200
000013
km/h
N
TRIP
0
1
2
3
4
5
6
7
8
9
10
11
12
13
x1000r/min
LOCK
IGNITION

KAWASAKI KLE500

Kawasaki's KLE500 might not be the obvious choice for anyone looking for a serious globetrotting machine. Unlike the Honda Transalp, the BMW GS and the KTM Adventure, it is far from being a legend in its field.

It does, however, offer no-frills, dual-purpose transport at a reasonable price and uses the reliable 500-cc twin-cylinder engine from the firm's ER-5 middleweight street bike. Although by no means fast or sharp-handling, this is a versatile, no-nonsense machine.

Available in only two colour combinations – titanium silver metallic or black with a deep, copper-coloured frame and black, wire wheel rims – the KLE gives an impression of overall ruggedness consistent with the role it is intended to play.

There are brush guards to protect the rider's hands off-road, small, flexible indicators that should withstand minor spills, and a well-padded but narrow dual seat for ease of manoeuvrability. Dimpled seat material provides leg grip when the rider is standing in off-road situations.

The neat handlebar fairing, inspired by the look of the Z1000 road bike and integral with the KLE's fuel tank, is said to feature a patented 'air curtain' design that displaces air around the rider's body at cruising speeds.

A strong, alloy bash plate protects the engine, front frame tubes, and exhaust downpipes from rock damage, while the high-level silencers are tucked well out of harm's way, to provide maximum ground clearance.

In keeping with the latest Euro II emission standards, the KLE has catalytic converters in both header pipes and another in the manifold.

Engine
498 cc, liquid-cooled, double-overhead-camshaft, twin-cylinder, four-stroke
Power
34 kW (45 bhp) @ 7500 rpm
Torque
43 Nm (32 ft lb) @ 6000 rpm
Gearbox
Six-speed
Final drive
Chain
Weight
182 kg (401 lb)
Top speed
169 km/h (105 mph)

KAWASAKI KLV1000

Any similarities with Suzuki's 1000-cc V-Strom, also seen in this section, are entirely intentional, for the KLV1000 is essentially the same machine, rebadged and re-liveried Kawasaki-style. It is the boldest demonstration of the partnership that was entered into by the two companies in 2001, when they agreed to work together on product development and production.

The KLV1000 was an easy way for Kawasaki to try to capture a slice of the ever more important adventure sports market that it would otherwise have been left out of. The only difference between this bike and the Suzuki are different instruments and a minor alteration to the fairing, which is improved on the Kawasaki by the inclusion of an adjustable screen.

Engine
996 cc, liquid-cooled, fuel-injected, double-overhead-camshaft, 90-degree v-twin, four-stroke
Power
73 kW (98 bhp) @ 7600 rpm
Torque
101 Nm (74 ft lb) @ 6400 rpm
Gearbox
Six-speed
Final drive
Chain
Weight
207 kg (456 lb)
Top speed
225 km/h (140 mph)

KLV1000
Kawasaki

KLV1000
Kawasaki

KTM 950 ADVENTURE

Engine
942 cc, liquid-cooled, v-twin, eight-valve, four-stroke
Power
66 kW (89bhp) @ 8300 rpm
Torque
81 Nm (60 ft lb) @ 6800 rpm
Gearbox
Six-speed
Final drive
Chain
Weight
198 kg (437 lb)
Top speed
225 km/h (140mph)

KTM's 950 Adventure is the king of adventure sports motorcycles – so much so that it almost fails to qualify for the category by being too much of a hard-core desert blaster and not enough of a dual-purpose machine.

The ones you will find on the showroom floor at your nearest KTM dealership barely differ from the factory 'rally raid' bikes that have performed so effectively in gruelling events such as the Paris–Dakar. The production versions are simply quieter, more finely finished and not so purely functional.

All the same, you could probably take any 950 Adventure straight from the showroom and ride it across the desert of your choice without trepidation. These motorcycles are beautifully engineered off-road machines that just happen to be road legal. Yet at the same time they are surprisingly forgiving to ride and so reliable that some even take on the role of courier bike.

The latest version concedes that not every rider is a giant by having a seat height of 86 cm (33.9 in.), 20 mm (0.8 in.) lower than on previous models. Even so, the S version, which has even more suspension travel than the 24.5 cm (9.6 in.) of the standard model, requires the rider to perch almost 90 cm (35.4 in.) off the ground.

Despite this physical size and the bulky appearance of the 950 Adventure's slab-sided fairing (which doubles as a fuel cell), this is among the lightest bikes in its class – and one of the most powerful. It produces massive torque and, in the right hands, can be incredibly agile.

Neat design touches abound, too. There is a usefully deep storage compartment beneath the dual seat and more than 2 litres (0.07 cu. ft) of space in the top of the dummy fuel tank. Suspension settings can be adjusted manually, without tools, from the side of the machine.

The fuel cells, which extend downwards on either side of the bike, have twin filler caps and a capacity of 22 litres (4.8 gallons), sufficient to give the 950 Adventure a range of some 320 km (200 miles).

Inside the fairing cockpit, an analogue tachometer is paired with an LCD, multi-function instrument that shows speed on one readout and total distance and trip distance on another. This device also displays water temperature, remaining fuel range and time of day.

But it is in the engine department that the KTM seems most impressive. The LC8 power unit is brilliantly compact yet still has an electric starter, dry-sump lubrication, a hydraulic clutch, an electric carburettor de-icer and double overhead camshafts. For the serious adventure sports enthusiast, there is no other option.

For those looking for the big Adventure's versatility and off-road ability in a smaller package, KTM also offers a highly capable 640-cc single-cylinder version (pictured opposite top).

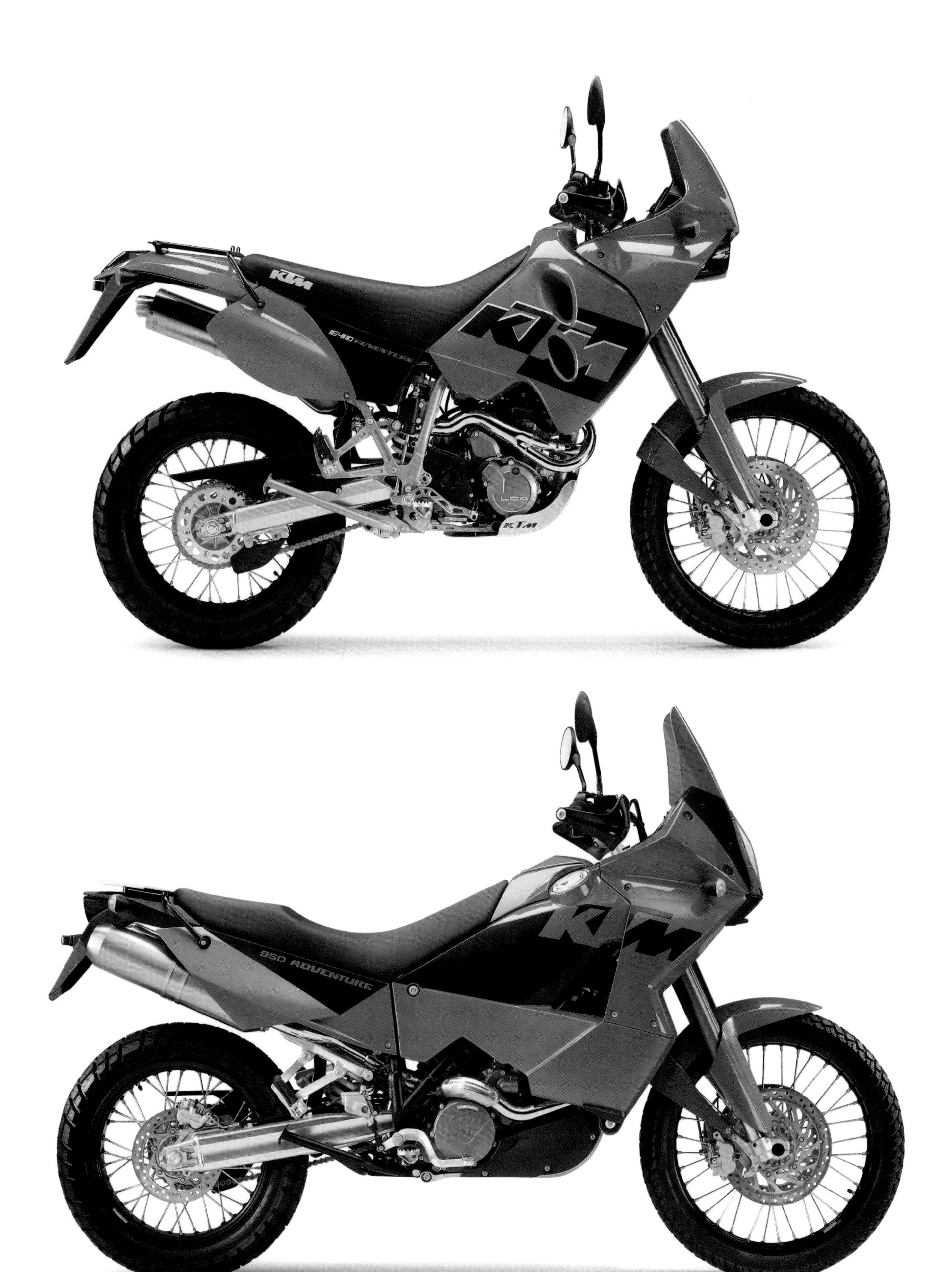
KTM
KTM
640 ADVENTURE
LC4
KTM
950 ADVENTURE

SUZUKI V-STROM DL1000 AND DL650

Engine
996 cc (DL 650 645 cc), liquid-cooled, fuel-injected, double- overhead-camshaft, 90-degree v-twin, four-stroke
Power
73 kW (98 bhp) @ 7600 rpm (50 kW/67 bhp @ 9000 rpm)
Torque
101 Nm (74 ft lb) @ 6400 rpm (60 Nm/44 ft lb @ 6400 rpm)
Gearbox
Six-speed
Final drive
Chain
Weight
208 kg (459 lb) (190 kg/419 lb)
Top speed
233 km/h (145 mph) (193 km/h/120 mph)

Suzuki's ultra-powerful V-Strom – not a misspelling of 'storm' but the name of a river in Bavaria – looks meaner than ever in its latest guise of all-black frame and swing arm offset by black or deep-blue bodywork.

One of the lighter Japanese 1-litre machines in the adventure sports class, the V-Strom DL1000 is still a comfortable bike with superb road-eating capabilities.

The v-twin engine, derived from Suzuki's defunct, Ducati-inspired TL1000 sports bike, produces tremendous torque, which makes it ideal for two-up, luggage-laden touring – and it scores highly over the TL1000 by having a 22-litre (4.8 gallons) fuel tank.

One of the great criticisms of the sports bike was that typical v-twin thirst combined with a pitifully small tank made it impractical for distance work. The V-Strom, however, can comfortably manage 322 km (200 miles) of cruising without refuelling.

And smaller riders need not feel intimidated by the V-Strom's size. Suzuki's engineers have gone to great lengths to keep the seat height low while retaining an ergonomic balance with the handlebars and fairing cockpit. The riding position is wonderfully comfortable, making for less rider fatigue and longer, safer journeys.

Keen to capture as much as possible of the growing adventure sports market, Suzuki now offers the V-Strom in a 650-cc version aimed at newly qualified riders or those who simply don't feel they need the 1000-cc model's output.

Using the SV650 engine, the baby V-Strom is still a punchy, powerful machine, enjoying, as it does, all the benefits of v-twin torque. Although physically little different from the larger machine, the DL 650 does have a seat height 20 mm (0.8 in.) lower and weighs 20 kg (44 lb) less. Fuel range is even better, thanks to lower consumption and a tank the same size as its big brother's.

Instrumentation on both machines is a rather clumsy mix of analog speedometer and tachometer and LCD fuel and temperature readouts.

The DL650, however, looks set for success in that it is the only Japanese competitor to Ducati's new 620 Multistrada. It is less expensive than all its 1000-cc peers, will probably be more reliable and easier to maintain than the Ducati and produces more than enough power to cover long distances. What is more, it offers big-bike comfort for two with middleweight running costs.

V-Strom

V-Strom

TRIUMPH
Tiger

Tiger

TRIUMPH TIGER

If you are seeking a three-cylinder adventure sports motorcycle, the choice is limited to just one machine: Triumph's beefy-looking Tiger. In this type of bike twin-cylinder powerplants are generally favoured for their narrow dimensions, but the Tiger's 955-cc, three-cylinder engine is sufficiently compact to make the bike look slim and manageable.

This latest version has revised suspension and steering geometry and a shorter wheelbase, all of which make it suitable for off-road use. Even so, like most machines in this category, the Tiger is designed to be a long-legged, comfortable distance-eater that can cope with an occasional off-road foray. It doesn't pretend to be an out-and-out dirt bike.

The Tiger stands out from the crowd thanks to its smooth, fluid lines, which are a pleasant antidote to the currently popular, angular styling of its peers. The softly curved, frame-mounted fairing – housing clear, white dial instruments showing revs, speed, water temperature and fuel level – flows harmoniously into a 24-litre (5.3 gallons) tank that gives the bike a potential range of 402 km (250 miles) on light throttle openings.

It also scores over its rivals by being the only machine in its class to be supplied, in most markets, with a pair of hard luggage cases as standard. These are moulded to the shape of the tucked-in, high-level silencers and this arrangement keeps the Tiger nice and slim at the back – a feature essential for both the cut and thrust of city commuting and for threading the bike through overgrown country lanes.

Engine
955 cc, liquid-cooled, double-overhead-camshaft, in-line three-cylinder
Power
78 kW (105 bhp) @ 9500 rpm
Torque
92 Nm (68 ft lb) @ 4500 rpm
Gearbox
Six-speed
Final drive
Chain
Weight
215 kg (474 lb)
Top speed
225 km/h (140 mph)

YAMAHA TDM900

Just as the long-forgotten two-stroke, twin-cylinder TDR250 anticipated the supermoto craze by a decade, Yamaha's TDM850 pretty much invented the road-biased adventure sports category when it was launched in 1990.

The trusty old liquid-cooled, parallel-twin engine has now grown to 900 cc and this latest version is endowed with the ever more popular extra of ABS .

However, the age of the basic design is beginning to show. Look at the unfashionable, low-level exhausts and the lengthy, slow-handling wheelbase, which is matched for quaintness by braking and suspension systems that are less high-tech than those of the TDM's competitors.

Yet this bike still has a great deal to offer. The engine may be old, but this is still the only machine in its class to benefit from a five-valve cylinder head and now, with the addition of fuel injection, it feels as fresh as any of its rivals, with lots of torque in mid-range, where it matters.

With an ergonomically excellent seat-to-handlebar-to-fairing arrangement, the TDM remains one of the most comfortable adventure sports bikes on the market and cruises effortlessly at 161 km/h (100 mph). A cleverly sculpted fuel tank looks smaller than it really is and provides a range in excess of 290 km (180 miles), while accommodation for both rider and passenger is wide, deep and comfortable.

It seems inevitable that before long the TDM will be dropped from Yamaha's range and replaced by a more state-of-the-art machine. This would be a shame, because it is an honest motorcycle that does a perfect job of delivering the goods to 'real world' riders.

Engine
897 cc, liquid-cooled, fuel-injected, double-overhead-camshaft, parallel-twin, ten-valve, four-stroke
Power
64 kW (86 bhp) @ 7500 rpm
Torque
89 Nm (66 ft lb) @ 6000 rpm
Gearbox
Six-speed
Final drive
Chain
Weight
190 kg (419 lb)
Top speed
201 km/h (125 mph)

Arai

Arai

YAMAHA XT660R

Engine
660 cc, liquid-cooled, single-cylinder, four-valve, four-stroke
Power
36 kW (48 bhp) @ 6000 rpm
Torque
58 Nm (43 ft lb) @ 5250 rpm
Gearbox
Five-speed
Final drive
Chain
Weight
165 kg (364 lb)
Top speed
164 km/h (102 mph)

Yamaha's XT500, launched in 1977, was the first Japanese 'thumper' – large-capacity, single-cylinder – trail bike. The XT model has remained in the range ever since, although numerous, carefully considered upgrades during its lifespan of more than a quarter of a century have led to the current model. This has a liquid-cooled engine, twin disc brakes, lots more power, quality, long-travel suspension and styling that is up-to-date yet remains unmistakably XT.

Although many still consider the XT to be a trail bike, it belongs in the adventure sports category for the simple reason that it has always been one of the most popular machines for long-distance travel to out-of-the-way places.

Relatively inexpensive to buy, basically bulletproof and very useful off-road, XTs as one variant or another must have conquered most points of the globe.

Despite its twin exhaust ports having given way to a pair of upswept silencers, the addition of a radiator for liquid cooling, a greater fuel capacity, a larger, considerably more powerful engine and a much higher specification than the original, the latest XT is actually far lighter thanks to the use of modern materials and computerized design.

This incarnation of the XT is, however, more suitable for use as a nippy in-town commuter machine than as a ready-for-adventure, long-distance touring bike. Nevertheless, plenty of after-market extras are already available, to make it more than a match for the naturally more off-roadable opposition.

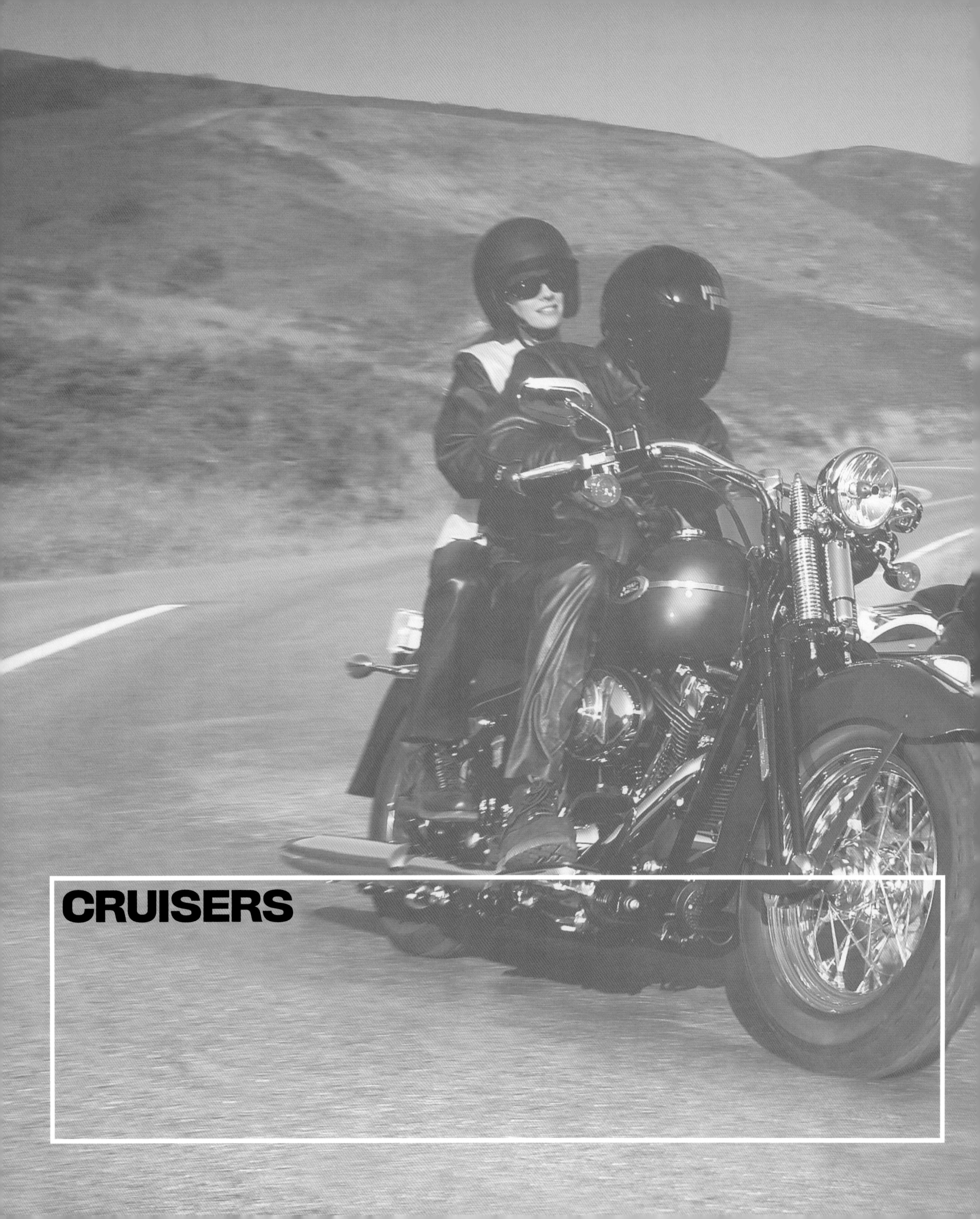

CRUISERS

BMW C1200 MONTAUK

Engine
1170 cc, air-cooled, single-overhead-camshaft, flat-twin, four-valve, four-stroke
Power
45 kW (61 bhp) @ 5000 rpm
Torque
98 Nm (72 ft lb) @ 3000 rpm
Gearbox
Five-speed
Final drive
Shaft
Weight
245 kg (540 lb)
Top speed
185 km/h (115 mph)

BMW's original cruiser, the C1200 Classic, burst on to our screens back in 1997, when it was used by James Bond (aka Pierce Brosnan) as an unlikely getaway vehicle. The Montauk, its name inspired by Long Island's Montauk Point, is the latest variant.

With its traditional air-cooled, flat-twin engine poking out of the sides, cartoon-like styling and an overstretched chassis, this motorcycle is not only very different but looks as though it might handle like a shopping trolley. Strangely enough, though, it is probably the smoothest, best-handling machine in the cruiser class and is one that needs to be ridden to be fully appreciated.

The fact that BMW makes a cruiser at all seems an anomaly since the brand is more associated with safe, sensible German engineering than wind-in-the-hair wild men cruising the highways on bad-boy choppers. However, the Montauk is meant to be, in the company's words, "modern, evolutionary ... and emotional", and it is. It really is a motorcycle that you just want to keep on riding, wherever the road takes you.

The flat-twin engine provides just as much torque as most of the v-twin opposition and, since it is tuned to produce a mere 45 kW (61 bhp), cruising is a wonderfully relaxed affair, leaving time to catch the glances of admirers checking out the Montauk's nifty styling.

To bolster the bike's beefy image, the front end is distinguished by an extra-fat tyre, offset by the twin lights mounted one above the other between the wide forks. A beautifully designed screen keeps draughts at bay, while the rider's deep saddle and separate pillion perch provide comfortable accommodation – the second even more so when an optional 'sissy bar' is fitted.

BMW can also claim to have created an unusual melody thanks to a combination of the Montauk's stubby silencers and an engine configuration unique for a cruiser, which gets a gratuitous dose of cruiser chrome in keeping with the machine's custom styling.

A final neat touch is the five-spoke 'italicized' wheel rims and the rear wheel's highlighting by a BMW roundel pressed into the centre of the left-hand hub.

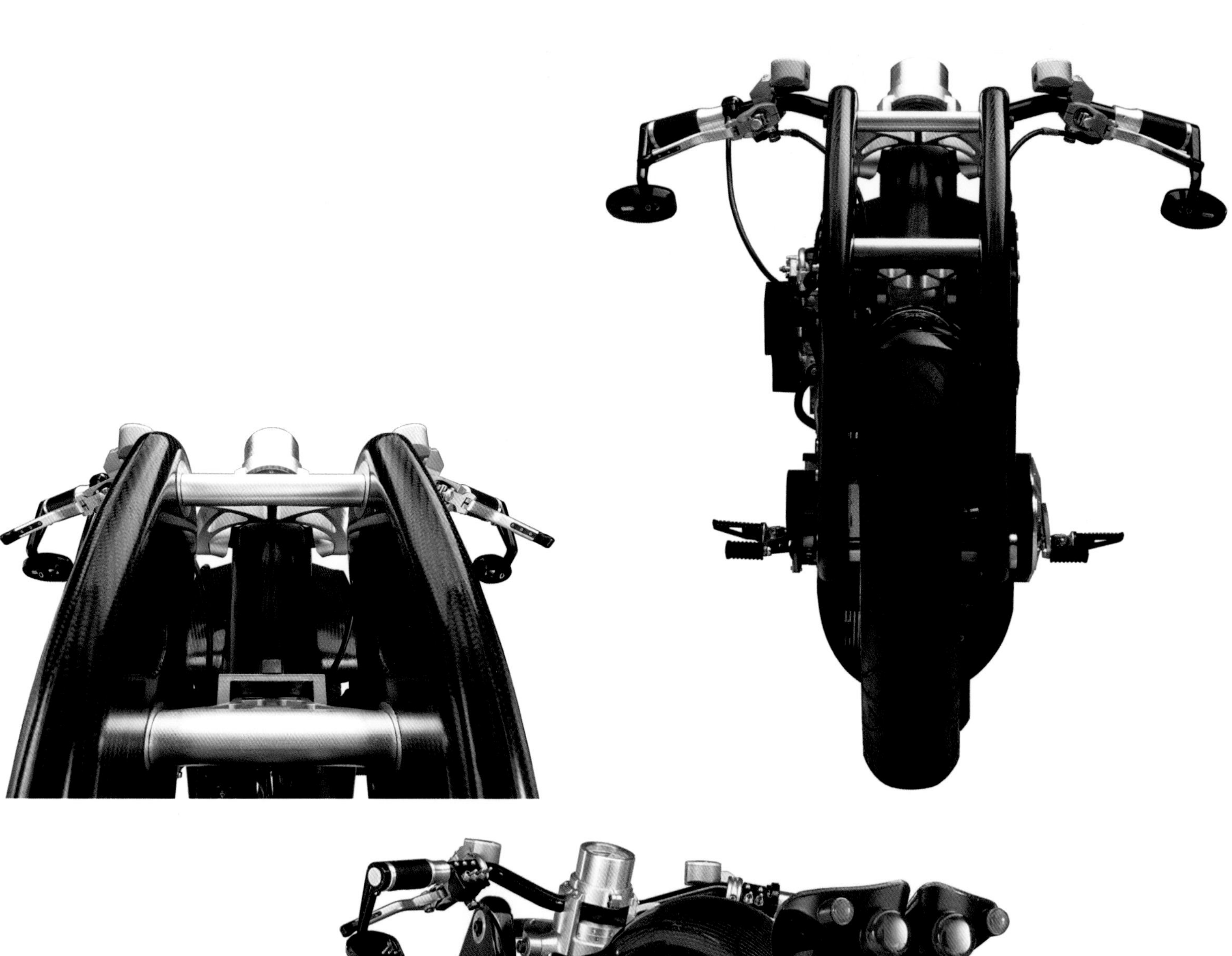

America has seen of late a surge in the popularity of radical-looking, hand-built custom motorcycles, due in no small part to the popularity of the Discovery Channel television programme *Monster Garage*, in which genius engineers with huge imaginations are filmed building outrageous vehicles.

The Confederate Wraith certainly wouldn't look out of place in an episode of the show, but the difference with this bike is that it is a genuine production machine, albeit one being built in very small numbers.

The first sixty Wraith buyers will be handed the keys to their wild-looking new toys at a hand-over ceremony in the New Orleans factory at the end of October 2005 – and what they will get is a motorcycle like no other.

The Wraith's designer is J.T. Nesbitt, a man from a different mould than most motorcycle builders. He takes much of his inspiration from the American artist and sculptor in metal Alexander Calder, whose perfectly balanced mobiles embodied much the same philosophy as that behind the Wraith.

The most obviously different feature of the bike is the massive, rigid front fork that is linked to a pivoting wishbone mounted at the headstock with a shock absorber concealed inside the steering head. The giant, tubular backbone frame sweeps down to the back of the bike, where it helps to support a wafer-thin seat that hangs suspended over the single-sided swing arm.

Like its stablemate the Hellcat, the Wraith uses a 45-degree twin-cylinder engine that is based on a seven-cylinder radial engine from a Curtis aircraft. This is mounted significantly forward of the central axis to enhance front-end traction, while the fuel cell is housed beneath the powertrain.

This arrangement not only significantly increases mass centralization, but also reduces the effects of weight change as the fuel level drops. Confederate has also reduced unsprung weight – vital to ensure sharp handling – by using ultra-light, aerospace-quality materials such as carbon fibre, high-density forged steel and aircraft-grade aluminium.

All-up, the Wraith weighs a mere 186 kg (410 lb) and, in Nesbitt's words: "It handles like my Aprilia 250 sports bike."

CONFEDERATE WRAITH

Engine
1492 cc, twin-overhead-camshaft, v-twin
Power
89 kW (120 bhp) at 6000 rpm (est.)
Torque
129 Nm (95 ft lb) at 5000 rpm (est.)
Gearbox
Five-speed
Final drive
Chain
Weight
186 kg (410 lb)
Top speed
Not available

DREAMCRAFT STUDIOS DCS-001 SAGA

Engine
1449 cc, air-cooled, v-twin, four-stroke
Power
47 kW (63 bhp) @ 5500 rpm
Torque
92 Nm (68 ft lb) @ 3500 rpm
Gearbox
Five-speed
Final drive
Belt
Weight
315 kg (695 lb)
Top speed
169 km/h (105 mph)

At around £150,000 the DCS-001 Saga must be one of the most expensive motorcycles ever made this side of a Grand Prix racer. This remarkable example of 'rolling art', which at first appears to be little more than an engine hanging from a pair of curving tubes with a wheel at each end, is the creation of California-based engineer Larry Nagel and designer Paul Yang.

Far from being long-time working partners, the pair met only in mid-2002 after Yang answered a postcard advertisement pinned on the noticeboard at the Art Center College of Design in Pasadena. It read: "Wanted: designer to help design a concept motorcycle. Call Larry, Dreamcraft Studios."

The most obvious feature of the 315-kg (695 lb) Saga, which took seven months to construct, is its lack of metal or plastic bodywork. It uses a frame that, as well as being the structural backbone of the machine, also provides its overall form.

Fuel is carried in a transparent tank and the engine (a standard, factory-built Harley-Davidson unit is used for reliability) hangs from the curving frame tubes on four massive, steel 'axles'.

Three slim, metal rods, cushioned by a trio of miniature, nitrogen-filled shock absorbers, give vertical support to the seat, creating the impression that the rider is floating on air. The triple headlights and matching rear lights are blended into the frame tubes.

The hand-made, crossover handlebars conceal all the operating cables and electrical wiring, with the right-hand lever operating both the front and rear brakes simultaneously through a balancing valve system. The left-hand lever operates a hydraulic clutch, with gear changes being made by means of a pair of buttons that activate a compressed-air shifter.

As outrageous as the Saga looks, it is said to be surprisingly practical and comfortable to ride. Even so, its wildly angled and stretched front end must make it no fun at all on the twisting back roads beloved of sports-bike riders. No more than six examples are expected to be made.

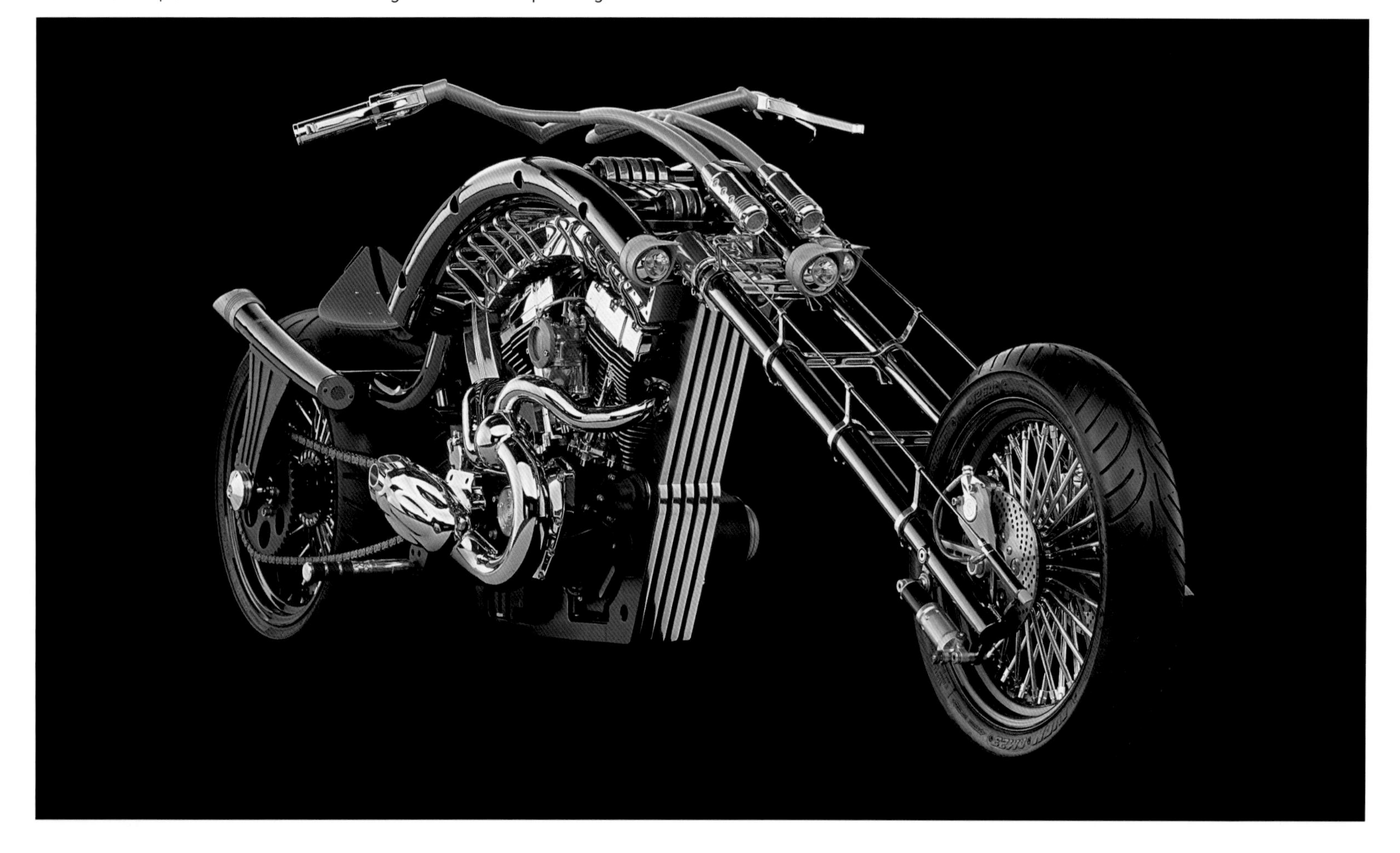

HARLEY-DAVIDSON FLSTNI SOFTAIL DELUXE

Engine
1449 cc, air-cooled,twin-camshaft, 45-degree v-twin, two-valve (push-rod-operated), four-stroke
Power
56 kW (75 bhp) @ 5500 rpm
Torque
103 Nm (76 ft lb) @ 3500 rpm
Gearbox
Five-speed
Final drive
Belt
Weight
322 kg (710 lb)
Top speed
177 km/h (110 mph)

Harley-Davidson has hit upon such a winning formula that it rarely needs to trouble itself with creating entirely new engines, chassis or designs. It simply has to announce a new paint scheme or cloisonné-enamel tank badge and its millions of followers throughout the world prick up their ears in excitement.

The new FLSTNI Softail Deluxe (not to be confused with the Softail Standard, Deuce, Springer or Heritage models) offers a little more than that, however. This bike is so retro-cool that it wouldn't look out of place chasing a Marlon Brando clone in a twenty-first-century remake of *The Wild One*.

Dripping with nostalgic styling cues from several notable Harley eras, the new Softail luggage rack turns a practical piece of ironwork into a sculpture with its gently tapered horizontal rails. The low-slung seat has 1950s-style chequered stitching on its sides, to complement the whitewall tyres, which became all the rage during the same decade.

Chrome detailing abounds, from the sliver of trim on the fat front mudguard to the 'bullet' turn indicators and the 'tombstone' rear-light fitting. The shiny theme is picked up again in the heavily laced, chrome-rimmed wheels, the trim of the tapered footboards and the chromed oil tank, which sits in close, contrasting dramatically with the black-painted engine.

With its lowered suspension and lazy, grumbling 1449-cc engine, the Softail offers typical Harley cruiser performance. It doesn't need to go fast. Just by being there it blows away the competition.

HARLEY-DAVIDSON

HARLEY-DAVIDSON FLSTSCI SPRINGER

Engine
1449 cc, air-cooled, twin-camshaft, 45-degree v-twin, two-valve (push-rod-operated), four-stroke
Power
56 kW (75 bhp) @ 5500 rpm
Torque
103 Nm (76 ft lb) @ 3500 rpm
Gearbox
Five-speed
Final drive
Belt
Weight
322 kg (710 lb)
Top speed
177 km/h (110 mph)

Perhaps the most immediate feature one notices on a Harley Springer is the component that gives it its name. The term 'Springer' derives from the archaic front-suspension arrangement, which comprises a pair of slim, girder forks that pivot against each other and are damped by a pair of central springs mounted beneath the headlight.

It might make for pre-war handling characteristics, but to Harley aficionados the Springer suspension is sacred and marks out the model as one of the coolest in the company's range.

This latest take on the Springer theme harks back to the famous 'Panhead' model of 1948 in having black-painted front suspension offset by a chrome shock absorber and springs.

Instead of the usual pair of mufflers running along the right-hand side of the bike, this Harley reintroduces the old-style crossover exhaust, which has a silencer on each flank, to balance out the look from the rear.

On a Harley such details mean a lot, as do the embossed nameplates that trim this model's seat and the vintage metal 'patent' label attached to the oil tank. Note also the fuel-tank-mounted speedometer, a Harley feature that has been around for more than half a century and has been endlessly copied by the original's many imitators.

To help the new Springer play its role as the ultimate lone-wolf cruiser, the pillion seat can be unclipped to turn the bike into a slick solo machine on which the rider needs just the throb of the v-twin engine for company.

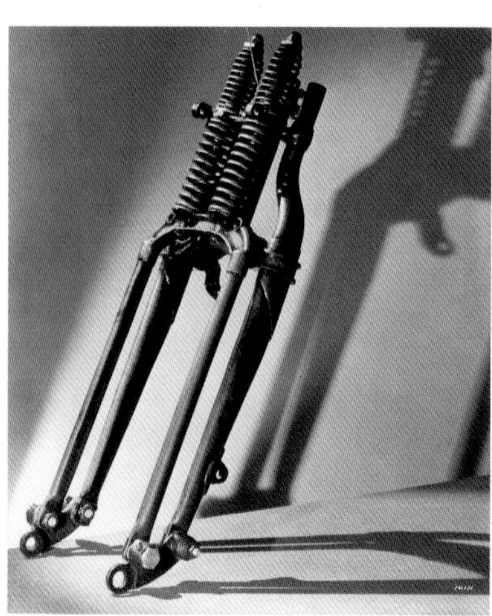

HARLEY-
DAVIDSON

JAN
48NX

Sportster

HARLEY-DAVIDSON SPORTSTER 883L (LOW)

Rather as Japanese electronics giants attempt to ensnare future customers by creating products for the young, so Harley-Davidson does the same by offering its Sportster at what is almost a loss-leading price. The aim is that people will buy into the Harley legend and either spend on accessories or get so hooked on the lifestyle that they go on to trade in their Sportster for a more glamorous model.

Yet, despite its entry-level status, the Sportster remains to many the very essence of what a Harley-Davidson should be about: a no-frills, low-slung, bad-ass machine.

Unsurprisingly, the Sportster Low is a Sportster with lowered and retuned suspension, mid-mounted foot controls and the new, rubber-mounted engine now standard on the model. Harley-Davidson has done this to make what is often perceived as a true biker's machine into an offering that will not, unlike its predecessors, intimidate novice riders, and that should also attract more women thanks to its lower seat height and easy handling.

Engine
883 cc, air-cooled, rubber-mounted, v-twin, four-stroke
Power
41 kW (55 bhp) @ 5000 rpm
Torque
65 Nm (48 ft lb) @ 4200 rpm
Gearbox
Five-speed
Final drive
Belt
Weight
251 kg (553 lb)
Top speed
153 km/h (95 mph)

CHIP SOLUTIONS
Infineon
CYCLE GEAR
Harley-Davidson

HARLEY-DAVIDSON VRSCB AND VRSCE V-ROD

When Harley-Davidson finally grew tired of constant ribbing about the stately performance of its traditional range of motorcycles, the company decided to show the world that it could make a machine that went, stopped and handled with the best of them.

The result was the VRSC V-Rod, an elongated, dragster of a road-going motorcycle powered by a Porsche-designed engine. In keeping with Harley tradition, the powerplant had to be a v-twin, but this is nothing like the rather archaic, air-cooled engine to be found in other Harleys. It has a 60-degree rather than 45-degree configuration, with liquid cooling, overhead camshafts and four valves per cylinder. In standard form this engine produces 86 kW (115 bhp) and can thrust the V-Rod 0.4 km (¼ mile) from a standing start in under 15 seconds.

Originally, V-Rods were available only in a distinctive get-up of brushed-aluminium fuel tank, solid-alloy wheels and silver frames, which all made for a machine that looked like something dropped to earth from an alien space station.

But now the VRSCB V-Rod has been introduced with a black-painted frame and a moody black paint finish to the tank, although the anodized-aluminium option is also available on the model. The minimalist instrument housing and the engine covers get the polished-chrome treatment, but everything else is dark and mysterious, down to the handlebar controls and brake calipers.

And, if the ripping acceleration of the standard V-Rod engine fails to provide sufficient excitement, Harley-Davidson's Custom Vehicle Operations (CVO) unit is now offering a tuned and tweaked version called the VRSCE V-Rod.

The engine is tuned to produce around 15% more power and torque, while the list of performance parts and trim extras runs to dozens of items, ranging from a 1250-cc big-bore kit to race exhausts, a heavy-duty clutch and neat, five-spoke "Reactor" wheels.

The hottest V-Rod comes in some cool colours, too, such as Candy Blue and Electric Orange.

Engine
1131 cc (VRSCE 1250 cc), liquid-cooled, 60-degree v-twin, four-valve, four-stroke
Power
86 kW (115 bhp) @ 8250 rpm
(95 kW/128 bhp @ 9000 rpm)
Torque
100 Nm (74 ft lb) @ 7000 rpm
(116 Nm/85 ft lb @ 7000 rpm)
Gearbox
Five-speed
Final drive
Belt
Weight
275 kg (605 lb)
Top speed
217 km/h (135 mph) (233 km/h/145 mph)

SUZUKI M800 INTRUDER

Engine
805 cc, liquid-cooled, double-overhead-camshaft, v-twin, four-stroke
Power
45 kW (60 bhp)
Torque
Not available
Gearbox
Five-speed
Final drive
Shaft
Weight
242 kg (534 lb)
Top speed
177 km/h (110 mph)

Suzuki's new Intruder seems, at first glance, to be just another cruiser – but look closely and you'll see some interesting features. Starting at the front, the bike gets the high-tech, inverted forks more commonly seen on sports bikes. The wheels are minimalist, three-spoke, alloy items and the engine is unusually narrow and compact for a Japanese machine in this class.

Exhaust and silencer arrangements are pure Harley-Davidson, while the kick-tail rear mudguard is reminiscent of one of the American firm's early Sportster models. With a deep, individual seat for the rider and a long, low chassis, the Intruder should prove a comfortable road-eater at moderate cruising speeds, although the 805-cc v-twin engine is not the most exciting powerplant on the market, producing a gentle 45 kW (60 bhp).

Suzuki clearly intends this to be a direct competitor to Harley-Davidson's entry-level, 883-cc Sportster, although the Intruder's water-cooled engine makes it considerably more refined.

As with the Sportster, a comprehensive range of tuning parts and custom extras will be made available.

TRIUMPH ROCKET III

Engine
2294 cc, liquid-cooled, double-overhead-camshaft, twelve-valve, in-line three-cylinder
Power
104 kW (140 bhp) @ 5750 rpm
Torque
199 Nm (147 ft lb) @ 2500 rpm
Gearbox
Five-speed
Final drive
Shaft
Weight
320 kg (705 lb)
Top speed
217 km/h (135 mph)

A cruiser that can justifiably lay claim to having the largest engine of any current production motorcycle is already halfway to being a success, for in the big, bad world of cruisers ccs mean a lot.

The name "Rocket III" was originally used on a BSA three-cylinder sports bike back in the early 1970s, but that was a very different machine from Triumph's twenty-first-century behemoth. This bike also has a three-cylinder engine, but it displaces 2294 cc, punches out 104 kW (140 bhp) at a lazy 5750 rpm, and looks so gigantic that you wonder if you'll be able to ride it.

But of course you can, becauseTriumph's designers have cleverly succeeded in giving the Rocket III enormous presence without making it intimidating. The seat height is lower than that of many street bikes, there is more ground clearance than on anything else in its class, and most of the machine's 320-kg (705 lb) weight is carried down low, making for handling that is much better than that of most cruisers.

The Rocket III has even been endowed with a sensible amount of steering lock, making low-speed manoeuvres less frightening than on some of its rivals. High-speed manoeuvres are, however, far more interesting. The bike lives up to its name in the acceleration department, producing a stump-pulling torque figure of which the average tractor would not be ashamed: 199 Nm (147 ft lb) at a mere 2500 rpm.

Despite its massive dimensions, the bike's looks are almost understated. Chrome work has been restricted to the substantial plumbing of the three-into-three exhaust system, the rear suspension units, the instruments and the headlight. The seat is very much a saddle and pillion passengers have to be on extremely good terms with the rider.

The pull-back handlebars, saddle, and footrests make for an upright riding position that is more practical than those of some of the Rocket III's rivals, which demand a stretched-out posture that soon becomes uncomfortable at motorway speeds.

Owners of machines such as this want to stamp them with a personal touch, so Triumph offers a range of customizing accessories, including a variety of 'flame' paint jobs, alternative seats, 'sissy bars' and loud exhausts. Even with the standard exhausts, however, the word is that many Harley owners can already feel the ground shaking beneath their wheels.

TRIUMPH

TRIUMPH

TRIUMPH

TRIUMPH SPEEDMASTER AND AMERICA

The latest version of the Triumph Speedmaster is endowed with an 865-cc version of the Bonneville twin-cylinder engine, a change that brings it a little closer to living up to its name – although it's still not that speedy.

Machines such as the Speedmaster aren't about speed at all: they're about lazy Sunday afternoon rides with your favourite girl or boy, taking in the scenery and making the most of the sunshine.

This and the America, which retains the original 790-cc engine, are more practical than many of the more extreme, overstretched, over-chromed and overweight cruisers that come from Japan. Triumph's take offers more all-round usefulness in a laid-back package.

Handling and ground clearance are perfectly acceptable for the performance level, the seats are comfortable and steering lock is plentiful for town riding and daily commuting. These two machines are street bikes for the rider who wants a taste of the all-American look without buying the all-American motorcycle or settling for a Japanese pastiche.

Although both have engines derived from the Bonneville, the 360-degree firing order of the two cylinders has been altered to 270 degrees, giving a lazier, more loping engine note. The Speedmaster's unit has a satin-black finish to add to its brooding looks.

The America features a useful, 16.6-litre (3.7 gallons) fuel tank, stylish, slash-cut mufflers, wide-set front forks and an easy, 62-cm (24.4 in.) seat height. In a nod to the past, the pillion footrest hangers resemble the side-mounted tool boxes of the original 1960s Triumphs.

Engine
865 cc (America 790 cc), air-cooled, double-overhead-camshaft, parallel-twin, four-stroke
Power
40 kW (54 bhp) @ 6500 rpm
(45 kW/61 bhp @ 7400 rpm)
Torque
68 Nm (50 ft lb) @ 3500 rpm
(60 Nm/44 ft lb @ 3500 rpm)
Gearbox
Five-speed
Final drive
Chain
Weight
229kg (505 lb) (226kg/498 lb)
Top speed
177 km/h (110 mph) (est.)

VICTORY HAMMER

Engine
1634 cc, air- and oil-cooled, fuel-injected, single-overhead-camshaft, 50-degree v-twin, four-stroke
Power
63 kW (85 bhp) @ 5500 rpm
Torque
136 Nm (100 ft lb) @ 3500 rpm
Gearbox
Six-speed overdrive
Final drive
Belt
Weight
299 kg (659 lb)
Top speed
193 km/h (120 mph)

Victory is a young American motorcycle marque, founded in 1998, but it has entered the competitive cruiser market with all guns blazing. Its latest creation is the wholesome Hammer, a cruiser machine in the great tradition, with lines penned by the legendary custom-bike designer Arlen Ness.

Just as the Triumph Rocket III can claim to have the biggest engine in its class, the Hammer can claim something just as important in the excessive world of the cruiser. This machine runs the largest-section rear tyre ever fitted to a production motorcycle, 25 cm (10 in.) across the rim, and puts a strip of rubber on the road more than 30 cm (12 in.) wide.

With its classic cruiser configuration of a v-twin engine in a long, low chassis, the Hammer could easily have been just another Harley-Davidson clone, but there is far more to this bike than that.

For a start, the high-quality finish gives every example the appearance of a hand-made one-off on which hundreds of hours of care have been lavished. Second, the 1634-cc engine packs a healthy punch at low revs for optimum, effortless cruising through the sixth-gear overdrive. Last but not least, its knockout styling is good enough to convert even the most diehard critic of cruisers.

From the super-wide rear mudguard necessary to accommodate that huge back tyre, through the smoothly flowing seat and tank unit, to the pull-back handlebars and monster, slash-cut exhausts, this is a two-wheeled work of art. Available in a range of garish colours, such as metallic lime green or red and flames, the Victory Hammer looks set to bring a touch of California sunshine to the dullest parts of the world. And, of course, there is already a range of accessories with which to customize and personalize the Hammer so that it stands out from the crowd even more.

VICTORY
MOTORCYCLES

SUPERMOTOS

APRILIA SXV 450

Engine
448 cc (or 550 cc), liquid-cooled, fuel-injected, single-overhead-camshaft, 77-degree, v-twin, four-stroke
Power
48 kW (64 bhp) @ 13,500 rpm (est.) (54 kW/72 bhp est.)
Torque
Not available
Gearbox
Five-speed
Final drive
Chain
Weight
120 kg (265 lb) (est.)
Top speed
161 km/h (100 mph est.), depending on gearing

Just as the Japanese seem to have accepted that the supermoto craze is here to stay, Aprilia has rewritten the rulebook in the middleweight category (as the Austrian firm of KTM did earlier by establishing an all-new class with its 950 SM).

Rather than stick with the traditional, single-cylinder powerplants usually found in supermoto bikes of around 500-cc capacity, Aprilia has developed a brand-new, ultra-powerful, v-twin engine for the SXV, which is also available in motocross specification.

While the single-cylinder competition is left gasping at a maximum rpm figure of around 10,000, the 450-cc v-twin has been safely spun up to a heady 14,000 rpm, which means more potential power, a greater range in the gears, and, as a bonus, a fabulous exhaust note.

What is more, the bottom end of the motor has been deliberately over-engineered so that it can be converted to 550-cc capacity with an output of up to 54 kW (72 bhp).

Yet Aprilia's design team has managed to make the 77-degree v-twin engine smaller, lighter and more compact than many a single-cylinder unit. The use of lightweight materials such as magnesium and titanium has helped this, while the overall weight of the machine has come down to 120 kg (265 lb), thanks to the use of a light steel perimeter frame.

As *The New Motorcycle Yearbook* went to press, the street-legal version of this awesome machine – which has been dusting off the opposition in the Italian Supermoto GP – was still a promise waiting to be fulfilled. No doubt lights, silencing and all the other frills necessary to make the SXV street legal will be kept to a bare minimum.

What is essential, however, is that Aprilia maintain the off-road version's overall look. Its black, red and orange paint scheme and slim, triangulated rear end are design cues taken directly from the RSV Mille sports bike. The SXV looks lean, mean and aggressive and has the performance to back it up – this is the future of road-going, middleweight supermotos.

aprilia
aprilia

aprilia
aprilia
4

BETA ALP 4.0

Engine
349 cc, air-cooled, single-cylinder, four-valve, four-stroke
Power
20 kW (27 bhp) @ 6000 rpm
Torque
38 Nm (28 ft lb) @ 5500 rpm
Gearbox
Six-speed
Final drive
Chain
Weight
149 kg (328 lb)
Top speed
129 km/h (80 mph)

Suzuki used to make an excellent light-to-middleweight trail bike called the DR350 that is, sadly, no longer in production. Its engine, however, has found a new home in this equally effective supermoto-styled machine made by the Italian firm of Beta.

The Alp 4.0 has its roots in the competent Alp trail bike but rolls on fat, smaller-diameter supermoto wheels equipped with high-traction road tyres. Closely spaced gear ratios give the bike punchy acceleration and this, combined with its lithe dimensions, makes it excellent for cutting through traffic.

Back-road handling is good, too, although the non-adjustable Paioli front fork is not a match for the exotic racing units used by firms such as KTM. Essentially, this is a supermoto aimed at younger riders, particularly those in countries where power restrictions are applied to new licence holders; its adequate but modest 20 kW (27 bhp) output makes it ideal for novices.

With that tried-and-tested Suzuki engine at its heart, plenty of Italian flair in its design and excellent handling to boot, it is an interesting alternative to a Japanese 'entry-level' supermoto machine and, with a reasonable amount of care, should retain its attractive appearance.

Beta

Beta
Beta

BORILE B500 SUPERMOTO

Engine
487 cc, air-cooled, overhead-camshaft, four-valve, four-stroke
Power
41 kW (55 bhp) (est.) @ 5000 rpm
Torque
Not available
Gearbox
Five-speed
Final drive
Chain
Weight
112 kg (247 lb)
Top speed
161 km/h (100 mph)

Umberto Borile is the first to admit that visitors to his workshop near Venice will never find a computer programme for designing motorcycles nor, indeed, a computer to use one on. All Borile's work is done by eye and hand.

Judging by the look of his latest sculptural creation, the B500 Supermoto, Borile's methods seem to work. This machine is a beautifully finished, craftsman-built supermoto that is completely up to the minute in both looks and components.

At its heart is Borile's own, hand-assembled engine, a 487-cc, four-valve unit based on the highly successful Italian GM speedway motor. This punches out lots of low-down power, making the lightweight Borile capable of mixing it with some of the best of the mass-produced supermoto machines.

Suspension is supplied by two leading manufacturers, White Power and Marzocchi, the wheel hubs are the best Talon items and the brakes are from Brembo.

Minimalism is Borile's keyword and this is what gives the B500 its superb power-to-weight ratio. Even the twin-exhaust end silencers have been made pea-shooter small by the use of a secondary silencing system concealed nearer to the engine.

The Supermoto is expected to be on sale in spring 2007, but for those who can't wait to get their hands on a Borile masterpiece, the tiny Italian firm already offers the B500 CR street bike and the B651 scrambler, a practical and high-performance trail bike with styling inspired by the off-road motorcycles of the early 1970s.

BORILE
BORILE

BORILE

DERBI
PAIOLI

DERBI SENDA 125

The youth of today know what's cool, and the only type of machines young riders want to be seen on currently are supermotos. Many countries restrict under-eighteens to 125-cc motorcycles, so bikes such as the Derbi Senda are becoming ever more popular.

It may be powered by a diminutive 125-cc, four-stroke engine that gives a top speed of 113 km/h (70 mph), but the little Senda has the fat wheels, the high handlebars and the waspish profile to qualify as a real supermoto, while distinctive dual headlights ensure that it stands out from the pack.

And it's a tough little bike: with trail-type wheels fitted, two Sendas completed Spain's Rally Baja Aragón without a single breakdown, despite being the smallest machines entered for this gruelling competition.

The simplicity of its air-cooled engine, combined with a practical, stainless-steel exhaust system and alloy wheels, should make the Senda a durable machine – even in the hands of over-enthusiastic teenagers.

Engine
123 cc, air-cooled, single-cylinder, four-stroke
Power
9 kW (12 bhp) @ 8000 rpm
Torque
Not available
Gearbox
Five-speed
Final drive
Chain
Weight
105 kg (231 lb) (est.)
Top speed
113 km/h (70 mph)

HONDA FMX 650

Engine
644 cc, air-cooled, single-overhead-camshaft, single-cylinder, four-stroke
Power
28 kW (37 bhp) @ 5750 rpm
Torque
48 Nm (35 ft lb) @ 5000 rpm
Gearbox
Six-speed
Final drive
Chain
Weight
163 kg (359 lb)
Top speed
145 km/h (90 mph)

The Japanese manufacturers took so long to catch up with the supermoto craze that it was almost as if they thought it would go away. Yamaha was the first to eventually join the bandwagon with its XT660X, and now Suzuki and Honda have followed suit.

Like its direct rivals, however, Honda appears to have gone into this class somewhat timidly, not really matching the no-compromise machines from KTM or Husqvarna, for example. Perhaps that's why it calls the FMX 650 a "Fun Moto".

The bike produces an unremarkable 28 kW (37 bhp) from its long-established, non-fancy, air-cooled engine, so it's unlikely to take the laurels on the average tight, twisty supermoto circuit.

But in terms of looks it's a definite winner. The black-rimmed, spoked wheels and the attacking profile of the mudguard–fuel tank–seat configuration give it the appearance of a machine much meaner than it really is. The chunky, inverted forks – shielded by black stone protectors – LED tail light and beautiful, slim, snaking exhausts, which end in neat, underseat silencers, add to the cool image.

Ironically, anyone who wanted a Japanese supermoto-style bike two or three years ago had to convert a trail bike by swapping the off-road wheels for some smaller-diameter, wider, road items. The FMX 650, however, might prove itself to be a handy trail bike if the swap is made in reverse.

Its fairly 'soft' – not highly tuned – engine, decent ground clearance, slim profile and engine bash plate make it ideal for some light green-laning. In its stock 'supermoto lite' guise, however, it is certainly a useful town machine, although it is a little short on practical touches – there is no luggage rack and no storage space and a minuscule, 10-litre (2.2 gallons) fuel tank makes it a poor proposition for weekends away.

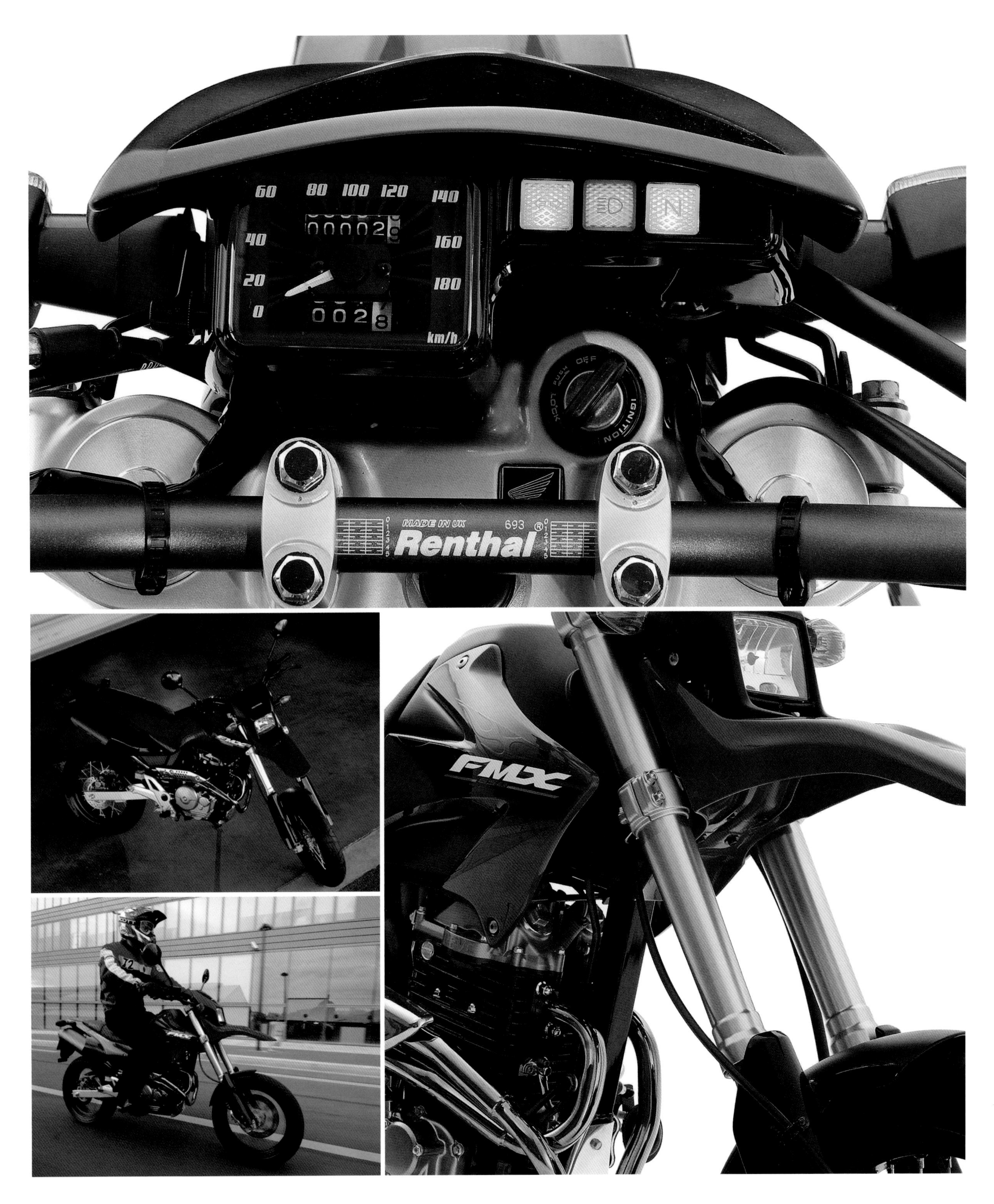

60
80
100
120
140
40
160
20
180
0
km/h
OFF
LOCK
IGNITION
MADE IN UK
693
Renthal
FMX

HUSQVARNA SM510R

Engine
501 cc, liquid-cooled, double-overhead-camshaft, single-cylinder, four-valve, four-stroke
Power
37 kW (50 bhp) @ 7000 rpm
Torque
Not available
Gearbox
Six-speed
Final drive
Chain
Weight
122 kg (269 lb)
Top speed
161 km/h (100 mph)

The Husqvarna SM510R can be ranked alongside other hard-core supermoto marques such as KTM. Although it is street legal, this is primarily a race machine and so does not prioritize comfort or practicality.

The seat is long and narrow and blends in with the fuel tank to allow the rider to reposition himself quickly and smoothly while banking the bike over on a tightly twisting track. The suspension is competition-hard, so riding on conventional roads in a conventional way is bone-jarring.

The SM510R's hawkish, streamlined looks are state-of-the-art for supermotos, from the 'duck-tail' rear mudguard to the conspicuous radiator shrouds beneath the fuel tank, which holds just 9 litres (2 gallons) – enough for around 129 km (80 miles).

The colours of Husqvarna's new bikes are different, too. Until now most of its models have been painted in the yellow and blue of the Swedish flag to denote the country where the company was founded in 1903. Since 1986, however, Husqvarna motorcycles have belonged to the Italian Cagiva group – a possible reason for the predominance of red on the SM510R.

Fast, featherlight steering requires just the merest input from the rider to make an instant direction change, while the 122-kg (269 lb) 501-cc, single-cylinder engine produces lots of mid-range power.

Wheelies can be called up at will in the first three gears, although the double overhead camshafts make for a more rev-happy engine than those found in the Husqvarna's single-cam rivals. And you can never lose the keys – there aren't any.

Husqvarna
SMR
MAGURA
SMR
SMR

KTM 450 SMR/525 SMR/625 SMC/ 660 SMC/640 LC4

Engines
625/654 cc, air-cooled, single-cylinder, four-valve, four-stroke
Power
40 kW (53/54 bhp) @ 8200 rpm
Torque
71/76 Nm (52/56 ft lb) (@ 5200 rpm
Gearbox
Five-speed
Final drive
Chain
Weight
131/149 kg (287/328 lb)
Top speed
161 km/h (100 mph)

In the world of off-road motorcycles the name of KTM, founded in 1953 in Austria, has become synonymous with the production of no-compromise machines of the highest quality fitted with the best components.

When the supermoto craze arrived, the firm used its years of experience in off-road competition to good advantage, quickly adapting its four-stroke motocross and enduro machines to SM specification with appropriate wheels, gearing and suspension.

But KTM supermotos are by no means mere conversions. Every model, from the raw, racetrack-only 450 SMR and 525 SMR to the sophisticated, liquid-cooled 640 LC4, is designed and built to meet the specific criteria of a supermoto racer. It must be quick, light and powerful, have superb handling, eye-popping brakes and, above all, be a scream to ride.

The firm claims that any one of its machines is ready for competition straight from the crate, and this applies to both the track-only SMR models and the road-going SMC and its slightly softer LC4 sibling.

The latest road models benefit from such styling tweaks as marginally smaller fuel tanks, redesigned tail sections and factory look-alike headlamp masks.

All models have the best racing brakes and hefty, inverted front forks and rear monoshocks by leading suspension manufacturer White Power.

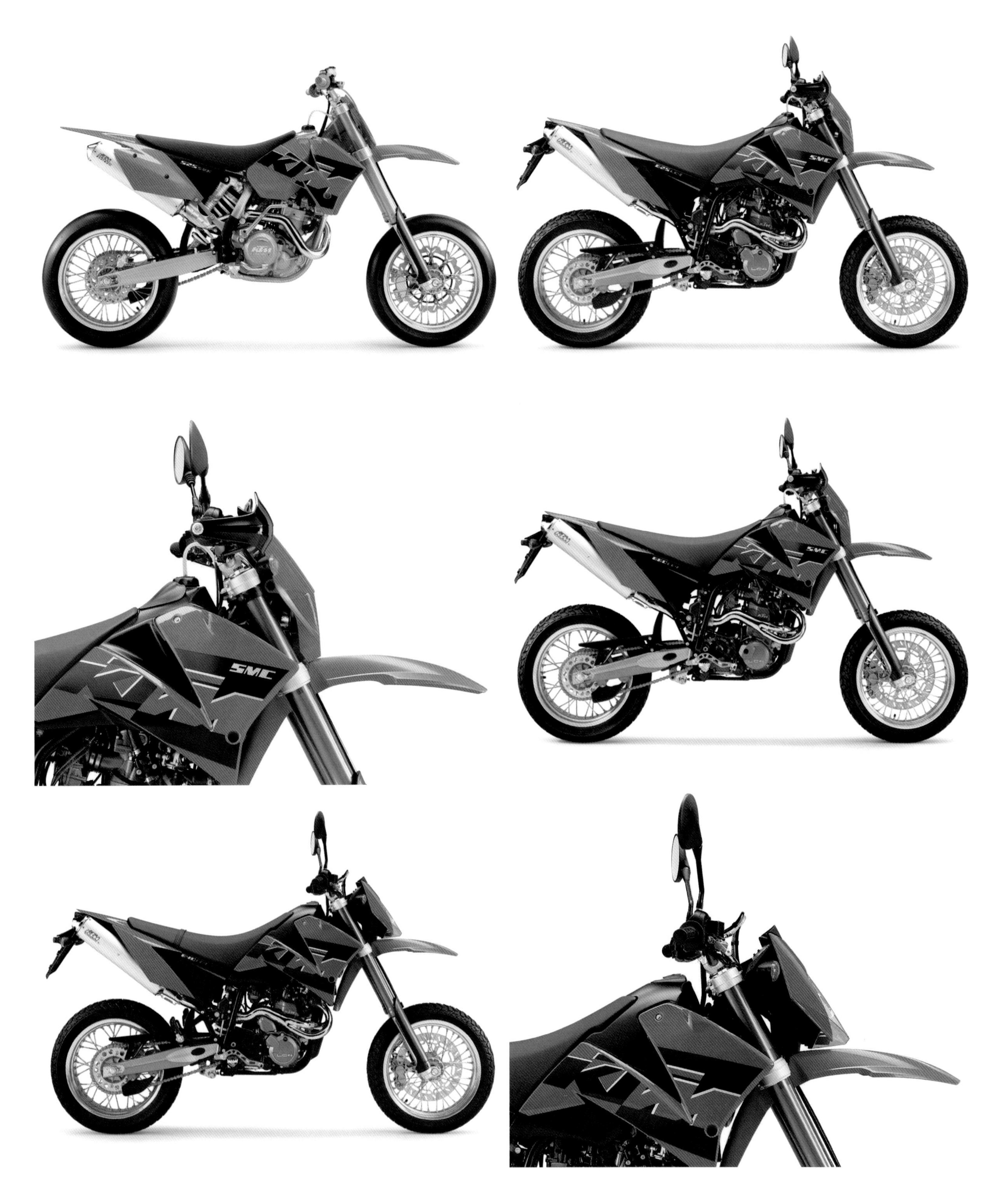

KTM 950 SUPERMOTO

Engine
942 cc, liquid-cooled, double-overhead-camshaft, 75-degree v-twin, four-stroke
Power
70 kW (94 bhp) @ 7000 rpm
Torque
90 Nm (66 ft lb) @ 7000 rpm
Gearbox
Six-speed
Final drive
Chain
Weight
189 kg (417 lb)
Top speed
225 km/h (140 mph)

Hard-core 'urban warrior' motorcyclists have favoured the KTM marque since it launched its Duke supermoto-inspired street bike in 1996, so it's no surprise that the Austrian firm now presents us with the most awesome supermoto machine yet to hit the market.

With a 950-cc engine punching out 70 kW (94 bhp) and housed in an ultra-light, powder-coated, chrome-molybdenum frame with the type of suspension and braking components that wouldn't look out of place on a Grand Prix racer, the KTM simply has no rival.

This bike scores over conventional, single-cylinder supermotos by offering a far smoother ride from its v-twin engine, which also makes it considerably more versatile – with a top speed of some 225 km/h (140 mph), this is effectively the first practical supermoto 'tourer'.

People who use it as such, however, are less likely to be making a trip to the beach than to the nearest mountain range blessed with smooth, twisting ribbons of road. With huge power throughout the rev range, pin-sharp handling, and the sharpest brakes going, the 950 offers back-road fun galore.

The slim profile and tall, high-visibility riding position, combined with the legendary reliability of KTMs (thanks to the use of best-quality components), mean the 950 should be a practical choice for the more mundane task of town and commuter riding.

But perhaps the most interesting aspect of the bike is that it is bound to force the competition to sit up and take notice – and then wonder why they didn't consider making a machine like this first. The 950 is an entirely new type of motorcycle, created by combining the popular traits of a big, punchy, v-twin engine with the nimble minimalism of a supermoto and the touring potential of an adventure sports bike.

The problem for everyone else is that the original is usually the best.

KTM

KTM

SUZUKI DR-Z400SM

Suzuki must have been surprised at the huge success of its DR-Z trail bike. The competitively priced combination of a reliable, reasonably powerful, light and compact four-stroke engine, a high-performance chassis and quality brakes and suspension made it an instant hit.

Before long, trail riders realized that the addition of road wheels and tyres to an otherwise stock DR-Z could turn it into a passable supermoto machine. Many such conversions have even made successful race bikes.

Now Suzuki has done the work for us. The SM variant has 17-in. (43.2 cm) wheel rims shod with high-adhesion sports tyres, inverted front forks and an aluminium swing arm as used on the RM-Z motocross machine.

Ultra-minimal styling has produced a tiny fuel tank that blends almost seamlessly into a long seat that lets the rider move about the machine quickly during the frequent and fast direction changes demanded by supermoto competition.

Large disc brakes make the DR-Z stop as well as it goes and, by paring everything down to the minimum, Suzuki has managed to create a bike that weighs a mere 134 kg (295 lb), not much heavier than most 125s and lighter than many.

Despite being a converted trail bike rather than a supermoto built from the ground up, the DR-Z400SM is serious competition for the likes of KTM and Husqvarna. And, being Japanese, this machine should prove reliable enough to be used for practical purposes during the week before being raced at the weekend – in the best tradition of budget motorcycle sport.

Engine
398 cc, liquid-cooled, double-overhead-camshaft, single-cylinder, four-stroke
Power
30 kW (40 bhp) @ 7000 rpm
Torque
39 Nm (29 ft lb) @ 5000 rpm
Gearbox
Five-speed
Final drive
Chain
Weight
134 kg (295 lb)
Top speed
145 km/h (90 mph)

SUZUKI

TERRA MODENA SX2

Engine
449 cc, liquid-cooled, gear-driven camshafts, single-cylinder, four-stroke
Power
43 kW (58 bhp)
Torque
Not available
Gearbox
Six-speed cassette unit
Final drive
Chain
Weight
118 kg (260 lb)
Top speed
145 km/h (90 mph)

Dario Calzavara, as the founder of the fledgling Italian bike-building firm Terra Modena, set out to produce a range of high-performance, single-cylinder machines of the highest engineering integrity and, by the look of the SX2, he is fully capable of doing exactly that.

Although intended as a street-legal machine, the SX2 is powered by the same engine as the Terra Modena supermoto race bike: a 450-cc unit that punches out a very impressive 43 kW (58 bhp).

With the bike weighing just 118 kg (260 lb) overall, this makes for the point-and-squirt acceleration and pin-sharp handling that are the hallmarks of a top-notch supermoto machine. A specially tailored electronic fuel-injection system enhanced by a unique aerofoil-fed airbox (seen for the first time on a motorcycle) ensures smooth and constant power delivery, fulfilling Calzavara's ambition that the Terra Modena SX2 should offer high performance but still be easy to ride.

The chassis is made entirely of lightweight aluminium and the bodywork is a combination of carbon fibre and Kevlar, the two materials most beloved of the racing world, while the even more exotic titanium also makes an appearance as part of the seat frame.

Top-of-the-range Ohlins suspension has been used front and rear, along with Marchesini ten-spoke alloy wheel rims. Further evidence of the bike's racing pedigree can be seen in its six-speed, cassette-type gearbox – and there are already plans to produce an automatic or semi-automatic, high-speed gear-shifting system for future models.

IWC
DUNLOP
elf

TRIP
km/h
ODO 000201

YAMAHA XT660X

Yamaha describes its supermoto XT660X as a "radical urban street machine". It isn't that radical, being merely the identical twin of the 'R' adventure/trail machine with a better front brake, replacement set of 17-in. (43.2 cm) aluminium wheel rims and road-going tyres, these items together adding 8 kg (17.6 lb) in weight.

Everything else is the same, from the small, streamlined headlamp fairing to the twin underseat exhausts. This is a bike for people who want either the supermoto look without the performance and discomfort of a more hard-core machine, or the practicalities of a trail bike – tall seating position, high, wide handlebars and a slim profile – for road use only.

What Yamaha should do is be totally honest about the similarity of the two ostensibly different machines and offer every XT660X with both sets of wheels, giving us two bikes for the price of one. Either that, or do what Suzuki have done: make a truly gritty supermoto bike.

Engine
660 cc, liquid-cooled, single-overhead camshaft, single-cylinder, four-stroke
Power
36 kW (48 bhp) @ 6000 rpm
Torque
58 Nm (43 ft lb) @ 5250 rpm
Gearbox
Six-speed
Final drive
Chain
Weight
173 kg (381 lb)
Top speed
161 km/h (100 mph)

RETRO

Norton
Norton

DUCATI SPORT CLASSIC

Engine
992 cc, air-cooled, overhead-camshaft, l-twin, two-valve (Desmodromically operated), four-stroke
Power
63 kW (84 bhp) @ 8000 rpm
Torque
85 Nm (63 ft lb) @ 6000 rpm
Gearbox
Six-speed
Final drive
Chain
Weight
193 kg (425 lb)
Top speed
209 km/h (130 mph)

They say that nostalgia isn't what it used to be. But there are times when it can be decidedly better, as in the case of Ducati's Sport Classic motorcycles .

Unveiled at the Tokyo show in October 1993, the Sport Classic range was originally intended to be no more than an experiment in combining the iconic looks of 1970s Ducatis with the latest in modern engineering.

However, such was the positive response to the concept bikes that the Bologna-based manufacturer decided to put the designs into production and make them available to buy from 2005.

Available in three variations on a theme, each machine in the range uses the same 1000-cc, l-twin engine mounted in Ducati's distinctive and taut-handling trellis frame. This attractive picture is completed by the addition of quality suspension and braking components, traditional-looking spoked wheels and iconic 1970s styling and paint colours.

First in the line-up is the Paul Smart 1000, a competition replica inspired by the long, low, 750-cc racer that Smart rode to a spectacular victory in the Imola 200 in 1972. The metal-flake silver paintwork and blue frame of the original bike – which was hastily put together from a hotch-potch of components found in the factory – has come to symbolize classic racing.

The twenty-first-century, street-legal incarnation of Smart's machine produces exactly the same power output as the original but with the greater tractability needed for road use, better handling and considerably better reliability.

Next comes the Sport 1000, a shameless single-seat 'café racer' in the great tradition that looks set to be the most popular in the range. Un-faired, with dropped handlebars and a black, stacked, twin-pipe exhaust system, it has, as a finishing touch, Ducati's classic Burnt Yellow paintwork on the sinuous curves of the fuel tank.

The third Sport Classic is the GT1000, more conservative in appearance and harking back to Ducati's tourers of the 1970s. The main difference with the GT1000, however, is that modern engineering should make it more suitable for, and more capable of, long-distance touring than its rather temperamental forebears. Available only in GT Grey complemented by chrome exhausts and a black frame, it is a motorcycle made for a tour down memory lane.

DUCATI

NORTON COMMANDO 952

Engine
961 cc, air-cooled, parallel-twin, two-valve (push-rod-operated), four-stroke
Power
60 kW (80 bhp) @ 9000 rpm
Torque
95 Nm (70 ft lb) @ 6500 rpm
Gearbox
Five-speed
Final drive
Chain
Weight
188 kg (414 lb)
Top speed
201 km/h (125 mph) (est.)

Until its demise in 1977 the original Norton company was one of the most revered names in motorcycling. Probably its best-known product – and also its last – was the famous Commando, an iconic sports model born during the mid-1960s.

The new Norton Commando 952 is the creation of an American firm based in Oregon that has no connection with the Norton of old other than the fact that the classic Commando was the inspiration behind this twenty-first-century interpretation.

Perhaps it is a case of auto-suggestion, but even without knowing that the 952 was a modern-day Norton one would immediately assume that it was, as it seems to have all the right lines in all the right places. It is what the original Commando would probably have become.

In creating the 952 the manufacturer's aim was to produce a stylish and powerful motorcycle that is also uncomplicated and simple to maintain. The parallel-twin configuration is just like that of the original, but much more powerful (the firm claims 60 kW/80 bhp at the back wheel). It is also likely to be considerably more reliable than the earlier engine.

The frame, which doubles as a reservoir for engine oil, is made from top-quality chrome-molybdenum in a traditional style, and the hefty box-section swing arm is supported by twin Ohlins shock absorbers that combine an authentic retro look with good handling capabilities.

The curvaceous fuel tank blends beautifully into a single seat that follows through to a smooth tailpiece reminiscent of the so-called 'fastback' design of the original Commando. The 952, however, adds a neat touch by having a faired-in rear light.

Norton aficionados will also appreciate the cone-ended megaphone silencer, which serves as an excellent replica of the exhausts that gave the 1960s Commandos their distinctive growl.

952
COMMANDO
Norton
Norton
OREGON
54586

ROYAL ENFIELD BULLET ELECTRA X

Engine
499 cc or 346 cc, air-cooled, single-cylinder, two-valve, four-stroke
Power
24 kW (32 bhp) or 21 kW (28 bhp) @ 5500 rpm
Torque
47 Nm (35 ft lb) @ 3500 rpm
Gearbox
Four- or five-speed
Final drive
Chain
Weight
73 kg (160 lb) or 77 kg (170 lb)
Top speed
129 km/h (80 mph)

The Royal Enfield Bullet holds the record for the motorcycle in longest continuous production, having remained almost unchanged since its debut in 1949. Originally built in Redditch, England, it was licensed for manufacture to an Indian company in 1955 and has been made there ever since, despite the closure of the British firm in 1970.

Ironically, the Bullet is now more popular in Britain than anywhere else outside India and is brought back to its roots by the UK importer Watsonian Squire. However, the model recently faced imminent demise as it seemed unlikely that its ancient engine would meet strict new EU regulations on emissions due to be implemented in 2006.

The bike's future is now assured, though, following the development of a new, lean-burn engine that retains the all-important look of the original. Dragging the Bullet all the further into the twenty-first century is a new, five-speed gearbox that was developed by a British engineer, and now the model even boasts electric starting.

Another significant modification to earlier versions is that the gear change and brake pedals have been switched from the traditional British set-up (the brake pedal on the left) to the now more familiar, opposite arrangement.

Other than the addition of a front hydraulic disc brake and one or two other, minor changes, the latest Bullet, the Electra X, really is exactly like the original from 1949 – which must make it the ultimate retro motorcycle.

The new Bullet is also available in stripped-down 'trials' form, as a totally 1960s-looking café racer and in 'full dress' guise with every available option, including single saddle, leather panniers, screen and crash bars.

ROYAL ENFIELD

ROYAL ENFIELD

ROYAL ENFIELD

TRIUMPH BONNEVILLE T100 AND THRUXTON 900

Engine
865 cc, air-cooled, double-overhead-camshaft, parallel-twin, four-stroke
Power
51 kW (68 bhp) @ 7250 rpm
Torque
72 Nm (53 ft lb) @ 5750 rpm
Gearbox
Five-speed
Final drive
Chain
Weight
205 kg (452 lb)
Top speed
193 km/h (120 mph)

There is no name more evocative of 1960s motorcycling than the Triumph Bonneville – and when the reborn marque announced in 2000 that a 'Bonnie' would once more feature in the line-up, nostalgic enthusiasts were soon queueing round the block to buy one.

The latest Bonneville T100 retains the essential retro styling of the original but features a bigger, torquier, 865-cc engine, as opposed to the 790-cc unit found in the more basic version.

Looks-wise, the big new Bonnie is just the same: bulbous fuel tank based closely on the 1960s original; sit-up-and-beg handlebars that combine a cool riding position with practicality; chunky, stepped wheel rims laced with simple spokes; traditional coil-spring shock absorbers; and, most importantly, twin exhausts ending in truly British-style silencers.

Although a world apart from the engines of the Bonneville of yore – which leaked oil, required a Herculean kick to start and vibrated like jelly – the powerplant in the reincarnation retains the same sculptural quality. It is, of course, much smoother, more powerful, more reliable and, hopefully, leak-free.

For those seeking to recapture the spirit of the 1960s in even greater detail, Triumph offers the Bonneville in 'café-racer' guise as the Thruxton. This version features dropped handlebars, rear-set footrests with slim, race-style brake and gear levers, minimalist headlight brackets and a sporty seat hump.

The silencers are of the 'megaphone'-style sports type and the paintwork – jet black, caspian blue or racing yellow – is offset by a distinctive, chequered band running the length of the fuel tank.

All it needs is a crossover leather jacket, white silk scarf and pudding-basin helmet and you're back with the rockers of forty years ago.

THRUXTON
900

THRUXTON
900

MAXI SCOOTERS

GILERA NEXUS 500

Engine
500 cc, liquid-cooled, fuel-injected, single-cylinder, four-stroke
Power
30 kW (40 bhp) @ 7500 rpm
Torque
43 Nm (32 ft lb) @ 5500 rpm
Gearbox
Automatic, belt-drive
Final drive
Direct
Weight
195 kg (430 lb)
Top speed
169 km/h (105 mph)

While most other makers of maxi scooters highlight the practical nature of their machines, Gilera has majored on the sporty side of its Nexus 500, marketing it as a hybrid that combines sports handling and performance with useful long-distance capability.

Roadholding and cornering are enhanced by the use of a 15-in. (38.1 cm) front and a 14-in. (35.6 cm) rear wheel shod with wide, radial tyres, while braking is taken care of by high-performance Brembo 'gold series' calipers operating on two front and one rear disc.

The 500-cc, liquid-cooled engine gives 161-km/h (100 mph) performance and, to emphasize the racy nature of the Nexus, Gilera provides a comprehensive instrument panel that records both the average speed and the maximum speed achieved.

The digital readout also gives information on coolant temperature, fuel level and range, average and current consumption and service status. A handlebar-mounted selector enables the rider to switch from one screen to another without having to release the controls.

Other neat touches include a set of fairing vents that direct warm air from the engine on to the rider's legs and a three-way adjustable seat that enables the bike's ergonomics to be customized to the requirements of each rider. Storage space in the seat is complemented by a fairing-mounted glove-box for carrying smaller items.

A recognition system built into the ignition prevents the scooter being started by 'hot wiring': the engine management system responds only if the correct key is inserted into the lock.

NEXUS
GILERA

HONDA FORZA-Z

Engine
249 cc, liquid-cooled, overhead-camshaft, single-cylinder, four-stroke
Power
16 kW (22 bhp) @ 7500 rpm
Torque
24 Nm (18 ft lb) @ 5500 rpm
Gearbox
V-Matic with electronic manual mode
Final drive
Belt
Weight
174 kg (384 lb)
Top speed
121 km/h (75 mph)

Honda's Forza-Z is aimed at the younger scooter rider who has graduated from machines of 125 cc or less but doesn't want to move to a traditional motorcycle. Therefore it has to project a cool and sporty image while retaining all the practical benefits that have made the maxi scooter so popular: ease of use, weather protection, generous storage space and a fair turn of speed.

The Forza-Z has all these, plus a few extra touches thrown in. It certainly looks great with its smoked visor, stepped 'bucket' seat, and tapered tailpiece that houses integrated driving and indicator lamps, while its 62-litre (2.2 cu. ft) storage capacity is the largest in the 250-cc scooter class.

But what really makes this machine interesting is its innovations. It is the first motorcycle to be fitted with a digitally encoded security system. This, instead of a conventional key, uses Honda's Smart Card Key System: the bike picks up a signal from a remote control carried by the owner, which means that he or she simply has to get on and turn a switch to start the engine. The system, which can operate from a distance of 2.5 metres (8.2 ft), is likely to become standard on other Honda models in the near future.

Another cutting-edge feature of the Forza-Z is its gearbox, which can be toggled from normal mode to 'sport' mode by a switch on the right-hand handlebar. In normal mode the automatic transmission adjusts itself according to engine revs and road speed, but by switching to 'sport' the rider can shift gear electronically between six ratios.

This is also the first scooter to feature a water- and vibration-resistant audio system that benefits directly from car technology by having a self-adjusting volume control that increases or decreases the sound output, depending on whether the scooter is accelerating on the open road or slowing down at a junction.

HONDA SILVER WING

Engine
582 cc, liquid-cooled, double-overhead-camshaft, parallel-twin, eight-valve, four-stroke
Power
37 kW (50 bhp) @ 7000 rpm
Torque
Not available
Gearbox
Automatic
Final drive
Shaft
Weight
225 kg (496 lb)
Top speed
177 km/h (110 mph)

The last time the name 'Silver Wing' appeared on the side of a Honda was back in the 1980s, when the Japanese manufacturer applied it to the 'full dress' faired and panniered version of its popular CX500 twin-cylinder, shaft-drive touring motorcycle.

Fast forward to the twenty-first century and 'Silver Wing' is the name of Honda's take on the maxi scooter, but this, while a 'mere' scooter, is faster, smoother and more comfortable than its motorcycle namesake.

Powered by a 582-cc, liquid-cooled, fuel-injected, twin-cylinder, four-stroke engine, the Silver Wing is capable of 177 km/h (110 mph), yet, like its competitors, achieves its performance through an easy-to-use, automatic transmission.

With handlebar-mounted front and rear brakes, it is every bit as easy to ride as a conventional, small-engined 'twist and go' scooter but has the acceleration and performance to make it a very capable road-eater.

Punching out 37 kW (50 bhp), the Silver Wing has been designed to tempt frustrated drivers out of their cars with its well-upholstered dual saddle, generous under-seat storage space (sufficient for several bags of groceries or two full-face helmets), softly purring engine and a very effective fairing that resists all but the severest of road spray.

A 14-in. (35.6 cm) front and 13-in. (33 cm) rear wheel make for a superbly handling machine that is a delight on sweeping bends at sensible speeds and provides a confidence-inspiring motorway ride. This is enhanced by a sophisticated anti-lock, linked braking system.

On the downside, the Silver Wing is, of necessity, large. It weighs a hefty 225 kg (496 lb) dry – just 10 kg (22 lb) less than Honda's 274-km/h (170 mph) CBR 1100 Super Blackbird sports tourer. Even so, it is remarkably easy to filter through city traffic, its bulk becoming noticeable only when it is 'paddled around' during parking manoeuvres.

Silver Wing
ABS

MALAGUTI SPIDER MAX GT500

Engine
459 cc, air-cooled, single-overhead-camshaft, four-valve, four-stroke
Power
30 kW (40 bhp) @ 7250 rpm
Torque
42 Nm (31 ft lb) @ 6000 rpm
Gearbox
Automatic
Final drive
Direct
Weight
219 kg (483 lb)
Top speed
129 km/h (80 mph)

Few maxi-scooter manufacturers would deny that they are keen to entice drivers away from four wheels and on to two, but Malaguti is more blatant about it than most, marketing its Spider Max GT500 as "combining the performance and user friendliness of an automatic motorcycle with the excitement of an open-top car".

That is a matter of opinion, but there is no denying that the Malaguti is a good-looking machine that is likely to turn as many heads as an open-top car. It is built around what the maker calls a 'V-Box' frame, which comprises a one-piece alloy backbone and headstock assembly designed along the lines of the 'beam' frames used in the construction of sports bikes.

A short swing arm connects directly to a 459-cc engine and priority has been given to maintaining a low centre of gravity, both to enhance the machine's handling and to provide maximum storage space.

In fact, the Spider Max boasts a 'boot' that is almost as large as that of some cars: it can swallow a pair of full-face crash helmets or a reasonable-size overnight bag. This is made possible by the fact that the scooter's rear bodywork flares out at the sides to form a 'boot lid' that is integral with the rear seat.

The one-piece fairing and leg shield assembly has deep, triangular side vents that circulate cooling air across the surface of the twin radiators. Inside the fairing, roomy storage lockers are built into the leg shields. Other practical touches include a sturdy ring that serves as an anchor point for a security lock and an engine cut-out that operates if the scooter falls over.

SPIDER
MAX GT500

SUZUKI AN650 BURGMAN EXECUTIVE

Engine
650 cc, liquid-cooled, fuel-injected, double-overhead-camshaft, twin-cylinder, four-stroke
Power
41 kW (55 bhp) @ 7000 rpm
Torque
62 Nm (46 ft lb) @ 5000 rpm
Gearbox
Automatic with five-speed manual override
Final drive
Belt
Weight
244 kg (538 lb)
Top speed
Not available

Suzuki's AN650 Burgman Executive (the luxurious version of the silver 650 Burgman shown below) is the maxi scooter equivalent of a well-appointed limousine. Available only in black, it has a powerful road presence that belies its scooter status and it offers supremely comfortable accommodation for both rider and passenger.

The seat is a generously upholstered two-part affair with twin backrests and the lengthy wheelbase of more than 1.5 metres (5 ft) ensures a velvet-smooth ride on bumpy surfaces.

Gadgets abound, including electrically adjustable mirrors, a height-adjustable screen and a sophisticated anti-lock braking system. The automatic transmission can be overridden in favour of a more sporty, manual shifter that gives five ratio options.

The Burgman Executive is also one of the most powerful maxi scooters on the market, punching out 41 kW (55 bhp) from its twin-cylinder, fuel-injected engine. This engine configuration is favoured by all the Japanese manufacturers of large-capacity scooters and it makes their products considerably more expensive than those of their Italian rivals. However, the reward is a much more refined machine that is capable of maintaining motorway cruising speeds seemingly without effort. A less expensive 400-cc version is also available.

BURGMAN 650
Executive
ABS

BURGMAN 400

YAMAHA T-MAX

Yamaha's T-Max was the first machine to combine the convenience of the maxi scooter with sharp handling. The manufacturer achieved this through the use of wheels that were larger than those of the average scooter and firm, high-quality suspension. Unusually, the T-Max also features sports-bike-style chain final drive, rather than the shaft or belt options more often used on big-engined scooters.

The latest version possesses what are perhaps the cleanest styling lines of all the super scooters currently on the market, with a coat of Midnight Black paintwork suiting the T-Max best. If you never believed a scooter could look mean and moody, now you know it can.

The T-Max is also the most fun to ride of the maxi scooters, combining the sporting nature of the Gilera with the smooth, fluid power of the twin-cylinder engine configuration that the Japanese seem to favour for this type of machine.

A generous airbox endows the T-Max with a throaty roar that further enhances its sporty feel, and the handling is still the best of the bunch. Yet, despite the trim looks and fun character, this machine is still a practical beast. Two crash helmets can be stored with ease beneath a large, comfortable seat that offers one of the most laid-back riding positions in its class.

The model is now available with anti-lock brakes. This is an important selling point for machines in this category as they are commonly bought by inexperienced riders who are looking for a safe, practical alternative to their car for daily commuting.

Engine
499 cc, liquid-cooled, double-overhead-camshaft, parallel-twin, four-valve, four-stroke
Power
33 kW (44 bhp) @ 7500 rpm
Torque
47.6 Nm (35 ft lb) @ 6250 rpm
Gearbox
Automatic
Final drive
Chain
Weight
205 kg (452 lb)
Top speed
177 km/h (110 mph)

YAMAHA

ODDBALLS

HONDA ZOOMER

Engine
50 cc, liquid-cooled, single-overhead-camshaft, single-cylinder, four-valve, four-stroke
Power
4 kW (5 bhp) @ 7500 rpm
Torque
5 Nm (4 ft lb) @ 4000 rpm
Gearbox
V-Matic belt drive
Final drive
Belt
Weight
84 kg (185 lb)
Top Speed
56–64 km/h (35–40 mph)

Japanese and American riders have been enjoying Honda's wacky Zoomer since 2002, but from early 2005 an updated version will be available to Europeans keen to sample the machine's unique styling and pure fun image.

Aimed squarely at teenaged riders and based around a tough, simple, aluminium and cast-steel frame, the Zoomer is the latest landmark in streetwise wheels, following on from inventions such as the skateboard and the BMX bicycle.

In fact, so relevant is street culture to the essence of the Zoomer that it has been designed with the ability to carry a skateboard in the cradle-shaped void below its saddle, a space that will also hold a sports bag full of kit.

Bodywork has been kept to a no-frills minimum to avoid costly repairs, but although the diminutive Zoomer is one of the smallest powered two-wheelers on the market, its 50-cc engine is bristling with technology.

It is the first scooter to be fitted with Honda's advanced Programmable Fuel Injection system (PGM – Fi), which makes the liquid-cooled, four-valve, four-stroke engine ultra-efficient and capable of achieving up to 70.9 kmpl (200 miles per gallon).

An Idle Air Control Valve (IACV) constantly monitors ambient air pressure and temperature to ensure the optimum amount of fuel is delivered for maximum efficiency. Although the Zoomer has a modest top speed of 56–64 km/h (35–40 mph), it has been designed to pull away strongly from a standing start in order to keep up with modern traffic.

A simple 'twist and go' automatic transmission makes the machine easy for a novice to ride, and maintenance is kept to a clean minimum by using a rubber 'v' belt, instead of a chain, to drive the rear wheel.

And, as you would expect of a machine designed to make the coolest possible statement on the street, the Zoomer's colour schemes are aimed at getting you noticed. It is available in Plasma Yellow, Fighting Red, Jet Black and, possibly the hippest of the lot, Camouflage Green.

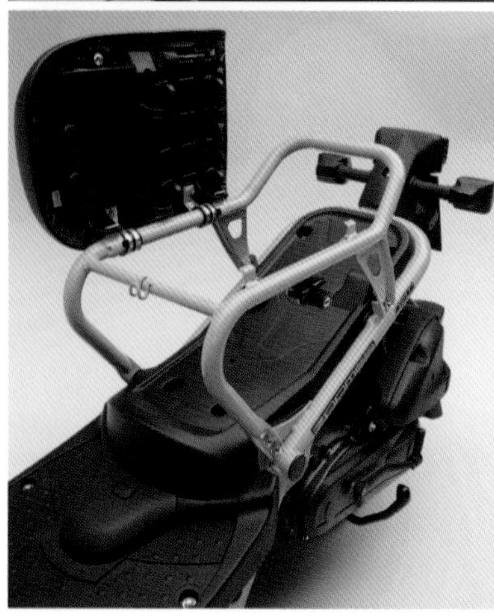

HONDA

SACHS MADASS 50/125

Engine
50 cc or 125 cc, air-cooled, overhead-camshaft, single-cylinder, four-stroke
Power
3 kW (4 bhp) @ 7500 rpm
(9 kW /12 bhp @ 7000 rpm)
Torque
3 Nm (2 ft lb) @ 4000 rpm
(8 Nm/6 ft lb @ 4500 rpm)
Gearbox
Four-speed
Final drive
Chain
Weight
85 kg (187 lb) (100 kg/220 lb)
Top speed
48 km/h (30 mph) (97 km/h/60 mph)

The Sachs MadAss heralds a new and imaginative approach to lightweight powered two-wheelers that fits in with the 'street culture' trend that popularized skateboards and BMX bicycles.

Pared down, wild-looking and designed with fun in mind, the MadAss is best described as a sturdy mountain-bike frame fitted with a horizontal engine, chunky wheels and sharp brakes.

Weighing a mere 85 kg (187 lb) in its 50-cc form, the MadAss has been designed to look cool when ridden normally, but even cooler when it is used for fancy stunts such as wheelies, stoppies (standing the bike on its nose through firm pressure on the front brake), and power slides. It is, essentially, a machine to show off with.

Equally, however, the MadAss is a practical means of transport, its slim dimensions and lack of weight making it easy to park in tight spaces – although its tiny saddle precludes sustained out-of-town use and, for the same reason, its passenger-carrying ability is strictly limited.

Sachs, a German firm that specializes in mopeds and lightweight motorcycles, also offers the MadAss with a 125-cc, four-stroke engine, but it further displayed the potential of the machine at the 2004 Intermot show by unveiling a beefed-up version powered by a 500-cc Royal Enfield engine.

Although this MadAss with added kick was only conceived as a concept bike for the amusement of visitors, it attracted considerable attention from the crowds. The bigger engine transforms the MadAss from an accessory of youth culture that most 'real' bikers might not take seriously into a covetable street machine that mixes ultra-modern looks with the classic sound and performance of a 500-cc 'thumper' engine.

If Sachs decides to put the concept bike into production there is no doubt that it would quickly attract a following.

YAMAHA PASSOL

Engine
Permanent magnet synchronous motor
Power
0.6 kW (0.8 bhp)
Torque
Not available
Final drive
Direct drive
Weight
45 kg (99 lb)
Top speed
40 km/h (25 mph)

We are always hearing about the car of the future that will run on anything from solar power to hydrogen fuel cells, but, aside from the few hybrid petrol/electric vehicles already on the market, motor manufacturers seem some way from marketing a viable alternative to the internal combustion engine.

And because petrol-engined motorcycles are highly efficient compared with cars – even a 274 km/h (170 mph) superbike will still achieve 18 kmpl (50 mpg) if ridden gently – there seems even less need to develop an environmentally friendly two-wheeler.

Yamaha, however, doesn't see it that way, a fact proved by the existence of the Passol electric scooter. This superbly practical little machine is the world's first vehicle to use a state-of-the-art lithium-ion battery that is small, light, quick-charging and long-lasting.

The whole machine weighs just 45 kg (99 lb), produces zero emissions, and, thanks to its electric motor, offers a totally 'linear' throttle response that makes it incredibly simple to ride. A machine of this type lends itself perfectly to electric power because, like a conventional petrol-engined moped, it will never be expected to undertake anything longer than an across-town journey.

Yamaha has already applied the lithium-ion powered electric motor to two other concept machines, too: the first is the sculptural Divide, a fold-up commuter bike, and the Pocke, another folding machine, which has space for a second battery but will still fit in a car boot.

YAMAHA

YAMAHA TRICKER AND TRICKER PRO

Engine
223 cc (Pro 249 cc), air-cooled, single-overhead-camshaft, single-cylinder, four-stroke
Power
16 kW (21 bhp) (Not available)
Torque
Not available
Gearbox
Five-speed
Final drive
Chain
Weight
95 kg (209 lb) (94 kg/207 lb)
Top speed
97 km/h (60 mph)

Yamaha's product manager Takeshi Higuchi was inspired to create the wild-looking Tricker by the concept of the 'X Games' and the popularity of extreme sports. He wanted it to be a combination of motorcycle and mountain bike, user-friendly and easy to ride so that even novices would be able to perform safely simple stunts in a short time.

The bike combines a light, short-wheelbase frame with the softly tuned and torquey 223-cc engine from the firm's popular Serrow trail bike. This makes controlled wheelies a simple matter of leaning back and opening the twist grip, while the design of the Tricker also makes it an easy machine to balance on while standing still.

The short-cut seat has been designed to allow the rider maximum body movement and nylon crash pads on the front and rear axles double as additional footrests, enabling accomplished riders to control the Tricker on one wheel or the other.

Tough suspension derived from Yamaha's motocross bikes ensures the Tricker can be used to perform spectacular jumps and its knobbly, off-road tyres won't clog up and lose grip.

Weight has been trimmed from the Tricker in every possible way – the mudguards are as minimal as they could get and, like the saddle, are made from ultra-light carbon fibre. The frame is entirely aluminium and fuel is stored in its top tube, while, for perfect balance, the main footrests are precisely positioned exactly halfway between the two wheel centres.

Even more radical is the Tricker Pro, with its engine and suspension designed for professional stunt riding.

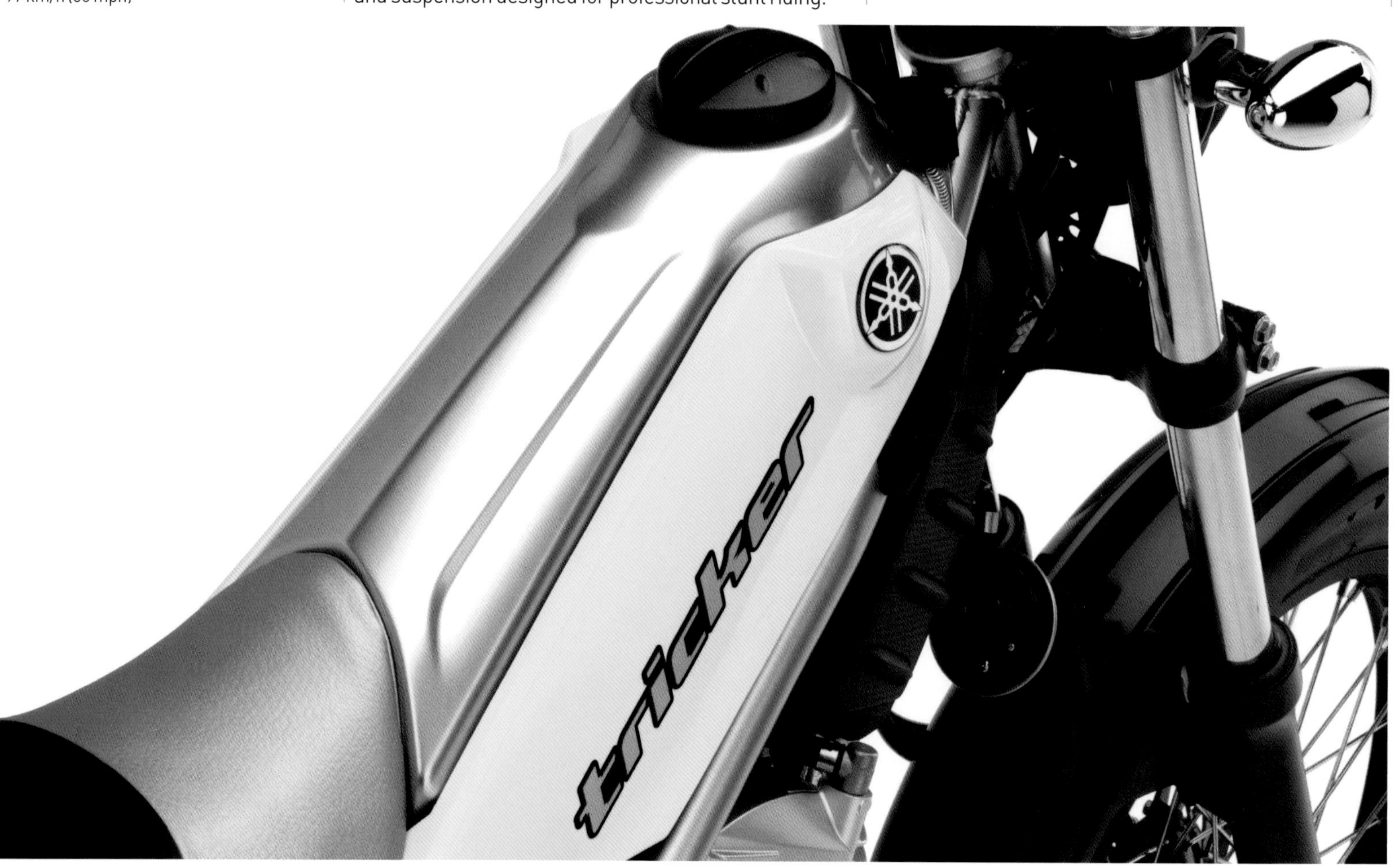

tricker

KEY DESIGNERS

DAVID ROBB

Vice President
BMW Motorcycle Design

Since BMW has a largely undeserved reputation for making rather sensible, staid motorcycles for the serious-minded, über-safety-conscious rider you might be surprised to learn that the head of its design team was heavily influenced by the psychedelic hot rod and beach buggy scene of '60s and '70s California.

David Robb first lived in the Sunshine State when he moved there with his parents at the age of 13 and so enjoyed the free-living atmosphere that he returned there independently after leaving High School in Michigan five years later in 1973.

"Back then I didn't even know what design was – I just knew I loved to draw and make models and that California was the place where I wanted to do it," recalls Robb.

"As soon as I arrived I enrolled for autoshop classes and learned how to tear engines apart and rebuild them. To make money I found work at a place called Walter Nettles's German Car Clinic which was a Volkswagen graveyard filled with acres of VW bug carcasses – my job was to find the part the customer wanted, take it off and sell it to them.

"The really fancy stuff came when I got the chance to help the mechanics, and that was when I started discovering all these amazing beach buggies and hot rods which still have an influence on my work even now."

As it turned out, his destiny in life was to design new vehicles rather than to fix old ones. He discovered his calling after being employed to illustrate private pilots' manuals. "Almost as soon as I started doing these technical illustrations I knew I had found my actual talent – and, even better, I discovered that there was a profession in it, too," says Robb.

This revelation saw him enroll at the prestigious Arts Centre College of Design in Pasadena from where he graduated with honours in 1979. The year before he had entered a competition for an internship at a major auto company – six were offering one place each, and Robb's obvious talent secured him the slot at Chrysler.

"A year later, however, Chrysler hit some very hard times and sent 20,000 employees home. I was one of them. I walked out of there with an unemployment cheque and went straight to the travel agency and bought an airplane ticket to Frankfurt.

"Once there I decided to tour Europe by train looking for work, and within two weeks I was lucky enough to have been given six different job offers with serious companies including Ford, Porsche, Audi and Opel."

Robb chose Audi, and spent the following four years working in the advanced design department on both the interiors and exteriors of the firm's cars before ending up as the in-house design consultant for VW in Brazil – where many of those California junkyard 'bugs' had started their lives years before.

"But destiny quickly took me back to Germany – I met my wife who had her own design studio in Munich and moved there with her in the mid-1980s. That's when I began to work with BMW, firstly with cars – but the way BMW motorcycles look has been all my fault since 1993!"

"The really fancy stuff came when I got the chance to help the mechanics, and that was when I started discovering all these amazing beach buggies and hot rods, which still have an influence on my work even now."
David Robb

Left
A design team member works on a large-scale rendering of the K1200 LT.
Above
The latter stages of a design drawing.

What Robb should be saying is that he has been responsible for changing the image of BMW motorcycles from being Teutonically functional and somewhat plain to being functional and often extremely interesting.

He and his 30-strong team have performed total re-vamps on class-leading machines such as the 'R' series flat twin tourers, the sportier K series fours and the GS series trail bikes. It is Robb's pen that helped establish the shape of the immensely capable R1150 GS Adventure and its latest dual-purpose stablemate the R1200 GS.

One of his most radical and forward-thinking designs was for an 'urban combat' motorcycle called the F650 CS, a single-cylinder motorcycle based on the F650 GS trail bike but intended primarily as an ultimate in-town commuter.

More than a century after the first motorcycle puttered down an unmetalled road, Robb and BMW finally addressed the question of how to design a motorcycle that would make light work of city traffic, have enough power for touring and also incorporate a variety of ingenious luggage options as opposed to them being added as afterthoughts.

It sounds simple, even obvious, but the 650 CS Scarver (for Street Carver) launched in 2001 represented a radical move for the German firm that sells many Scarvers to buyers who were previously non-motorcyclists but who are, in the words of the publicity campaign, "experience seekers".

To attract them to the Scarver, Robb drew his inspiration from worlds away from the traditional perception of motorcycles as being oily lumps of metal for hardened road warriors.

Drive to the rear wheel, for example, is not via a greasy chain but a clean rubber belt, which has deliberately been left exposed to highlight its practicality; parts of the swooping bodywork are made from the same type of soft-look opaque plastic used for the trendy shells of i-mac computers; panels can be mixed and matched in the style of a Smart car to change the machine's colour scheme, and the paint finish is sun-sensitive to pick up hues from other areas of the bike in differing light conditions.

The niftiest features of the Scarver, however, are to be found in its luggage system. Because it has an underseat petrol tank, the area between seat and handlebars normally reserved for fuel carrying has been integrated into the fairing and contains a central recess which is flanked by stout grab handles for the passenger and adapts to several uses, one of which is for holding a safety helmet.

The recess on the Scarver allows a helmet to be safely secured using flexible metal straps that are covered in rubber to protect visor and paintwork – they are also lockable, meaning the rider doesn't have to carry the cumbersome headgear once the bike has been parked.

In another mode, the recess holds one of two different sizes of handy, water-repellent soft bags

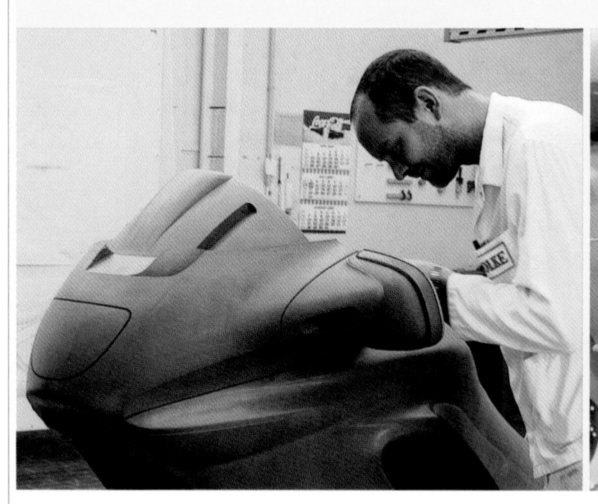

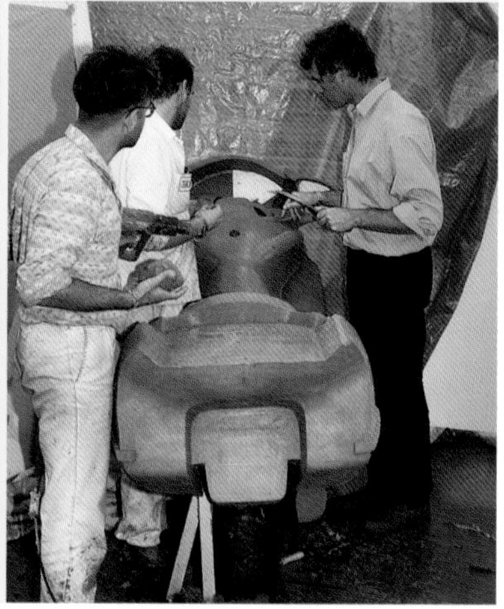

which can quickly be detached and used as holdalls; alternatively, a hard case can be fitted, or an audio system housed in a foam-lined carrier which has powerful twin speakers and connects to the machine's electrical supply with a single wire.

At the rear of the bike, a pair of zip-together bags which convert into a backpack fit securely to the integral parcel rack and give a combined carrying capacity of 35 litres – sufficient space even for those who refuse to recognize the phrase "travelling light".

"When we set out to design this bike, we asked ourselves two very simple questions: what type of person will buy it and why? " explained Robb.

"The answers we came up with were that they would be the type of people who like their possessions to make a fashionable statement and who like objects which are attractive but which work well on a practical level. This is not a motorcycle for the hard core biker – it is aimed at people who are looking for a means of getting through the city during the week, who want a machine which enhances their urban lifestyle and has useful features for day to day life, but which can take them off on adventures at the weekends."

When the Scarver was launched I remember asking Robb whether or not BMW had any plans to build a sports bike which could potentially compete with the best the Japanese had to offer. At the time the answer was an emphatic no – but check out the Sports Bike and Naked sections of this book and you'll see that, within four short years, the company's philosophy has clearly changed.

The K1200 S and its un-faired sibling the K1200 R both have immensely powerful engines and excellent handling which make them direct competition to what the Japanese have to offer.

"For some time now we have been working on bikes with similar platforms and changing body styles and details to create machines which have very different characters," explains Robb.

"With the K1200 R we are really pushing the envelope, but it is just one of several new directions which BMW motorcycles hopes to take. We are looking at all the options right now; some would seem pretty logical to people who know us and there is no way we'll be forgetting our very loyal core customer base.

"On the other hand we do have plans to move into a more dynamic area – and that means we will continue to look at motorcycles that really kick ass."

Left
A BMW design team member works on a K-series prototype.
Above
Fairings and luggage are not afterthoughts on BMW motorcycles: they are integral to the design concept.

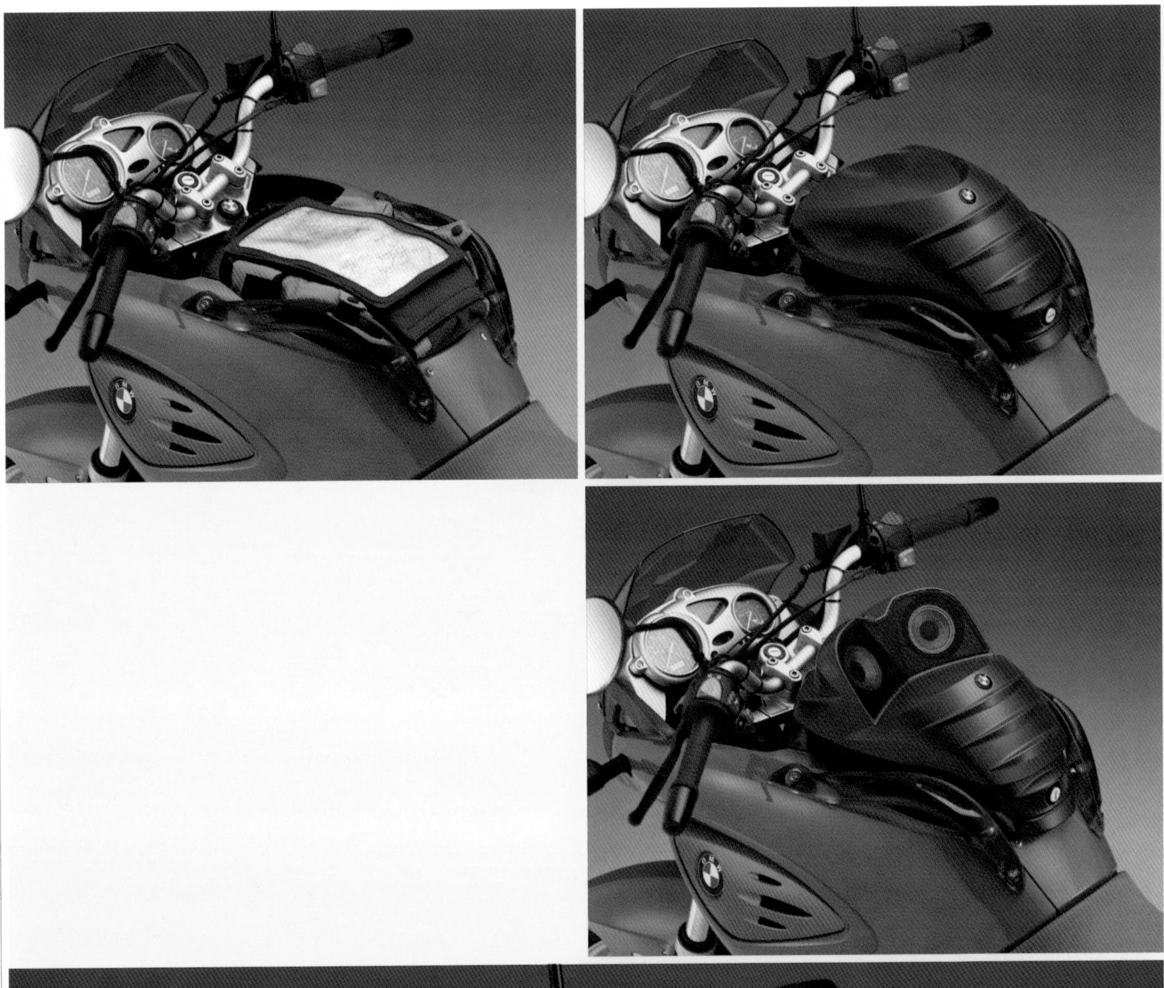

Left
The Robb-designed F650 CS features a 'dummy' fuel tank with a recess designed to hold everything from a crash helmet to a weatherproof audio system.

PIERRE TERBLANCHE

Director of Design
Ducati

There are plenty of things that can make a grown man cry, and a motorbike is one of them. I know this, because I saw it happen at a Ducati gathering in Las Vegas in 2001. Among the thousands of 'Ducatisti' who had turned up with their rumbling steeds was Michael Wozniak, a retired policeman from Oakland, California, who had travelled to the event with his coveted MH900E (for "Evoluzione") strapped securely to a trailer on the back of his car.

The MH900E was a landmark motorcycle for various reasons. A retro-styled machine created to pay tribute to the legendary Ducati racer the late Mike Hailwood, it was built in a strictly limited series of 2000.

Priced at 15,000 euros each, the bikes could be ordered only through the internet and not before one second after midnight on 1 January 2000. Like considerably more than 2000 other wealthy Ducati fans, Wozniak had sat with finger poised over his computer mouse to make certain that he got one of the first batch of the bikes, which sold out before dawn. He succeeded and, after taking delivery of the machine, he kept it on a pedestal in his living room.

Wozniak was happy to travel to Las Vegas to show off the MH to anyone who wanted to see it, but what he had never expected was that he would meet Pierre Terblanche, the Ducati chief designer who had created the model and who has subsequently designed the company's latest machines, such as the 999 and 749, the Multistrada and the Sport Classic range, all of which you will find in this book.

Terblanche made Wozniak's day by agreeing to sign the tailpiece of his MH with a silver marker pen made runny by the scorching sun. As an ex-cop the MH fan must have seen the harsher side of life, but he still couldn't hold back a tear as Terblanche struggled with the dribbling ink to apply his name in simple, un-joined-up letters to the shiny red paintwork.

"It was beyond my wildest dreams. I didn't expect him to be such a nice guy. I have fourteen other motorcycles but this is my favourite by leaps and bounds. It is like a beautiful sculpture and now I have met the man who actually designed it. It's unreal," gushed Wozniak.

Motorcycles can do that to people, and Ducatis in particular – so Terblanche is carrying an unenviable degree of responsibility as the man in charge of what the different bikes in the range get to look like.

Born in Uitenhage, South Africa, in 1956 and originally trained as a graphic designer, Pierre Terblanche began his career in advertising, working on the Ford Motors account with Young & Rubicam in Cape Town.

His passion for automotive styling led him to enrol for a master's degree in transport design at the Royal College of Art in London and after graduating he took a job in Volkswagen's advanced design studio, Design Düsseldorf, in Germany, where he worked on VW Golf interiors and the VW Polo project from 1986 to 1989.

In 1989 he joined Ducati Rimini, where he worked for two years with Massimo Tamburini on the Paso restyling as well as the 888 and the iconic 916. After three years

"I'm obviously aware that many people were surprised at the looks of the 999 and 749, and indeed the Multistrada, but the important thing is that a design should both work and make you think, and I believe that is what they do."
Pierre Terblanche

Opposite
Pierre Terblanche with a Ducati sports tourer.
Above
Terblanche with three of his creations.

he moved to the Cagiva design centre in Morazzone Varese, Italy, where he created the Cagiva 600 Enduro, called the "Canyon", and, more importantly, the landmark Ducati Supermono, which was heavily influenced by the look of the 916 and became one of the most important motorcycle designs of the modern era.

The Supermono, as the name suggests, was a single-cylinder racing bike. It had an engine capacity of 550 cc and was capable of a top speed in excess of 209 km/h (130 mph). Aerodynamics plays a very significant part in the performance of a machine such as this, which, while powerful for its class, does not have the brute force of a larger-engined racer.

As a result, the design of the fairing and bodywork – a project entrusted to Terblanche after the bike was conceived by Massimo Bordi and developed by engineer Claudio Domenicali – was crucial. The finished product not only looked beautiful but proved highly efficient too, helping the Supermono to become one of the most competitive single-cylinder race bikes of all time.

Terblanche joined Ducati as director of design in 1997 after the firm became independent, his first task in the job being to design the new Supersport 900 road bike. The following year the MHE900 Evoluzione was presented at the Munich Show and at the 2003 Tokyo Motorshow the Sport Classics were unveiled, initially as a design exercise. But, as you can see from the Retro section of this book, a favourable worldwide reaction to the bikes means that Ducati is going into production with all three models, starting with the Paul Smart Replica.

Nevertheless, it has not all been plain sailing for Terblanche, who shocked many Ducati fans with the 999. This, being the successor to the 998 (which looked almost identical to Massimo Tamburini's 916, believed by many to be the most beautiful motorcycle of all time) had an extremely hard act to follow.

In fact, huge numbers of Ducatisti have yet to come to terms with the looks of the 999 and many are also uncertain about the appearance of the Multistrada, although most agree that both bikes perform superbly.

The 999 was a logical progression from the 916 series, but the Multistrada was an entirely new machine for Ducati and indeed a new concept in motorcycling – its name marks it out as being a motorcycle "for all roads".

While not a trail bike, it has a trail bike's upright looks; while not a sports bike, it handles supremely; and while not a conventional tourer, it allows a rider to cover long distances at high speeds out of the wind blast, thanks to that controversial – and some say downright ugly – two-part fairing, the top half of which turns with the handlebars.

"I'm obviously aware that many people were surprised at the looks of the 999 and 749, and indeed the Multistrada, but the important thing is that a design should both work and make you think, and I believe that is what they do," says Terblanche.

"Because of the way a motorcycle is built, we, as designers, have to be involved in every aspect of its creation as the shape, size and position of every component is vital to the way the machine functions

as well as the way it looks. It is not the same as car design, where parts of the interior, for example, can be designed separately to the rest of the vehicle. On a motorcycle there is more interaction between components.

"All my designs start life as a hand drawing. I am constantly scribbling, whether I'm in a meeting, talking on the phone, or just sitting at my desk and when you're not specifically concentrating on designing something it is amazing what can naturally appear in front of you.

"At the moment the team is working on many new ideas for different types of motorcyles, some of which will be definitely emerging in the foreseeable future – for now, though, that is all I can say. There are lots of secrets."

What Terblanche can talk about, however, is the evolution of the trio of motorcycles that make up the forthcoming Sport Classic range. About these machines the world's motorcyclists seem to be in unanimous agreement: they look fabulous.

"They really stemmed from the MHE 900, which I designed five years ago," explains Terblanche.

"From the outset that was supposed to be the first bike in a family, and the next member of that family was the Paul Smart Replica, the race-styled bike with the wonderful metal-flake silver fuel tank which even includes a replica of a dead fly in the paintwork because one got mixed up in the paint on the original 1970s bike!" the designer remembers.

"The most difficult part of designing those bikes was to make them recall the old ones. If you parked one of the Sport Classics next to one of the originals you would instantly be able to see that the newer machine is a totally modern sports bike.

"They have all the latest componentry and build quality, yet we had to give it the look and spirit of the old machines – and, judging by the reaction they've received from around the world, it looks as though we might well have got the mixture right."

Left
An MH900E owner mounts up.
Right
Terblanche signs Michael Wozniak's pride and joy.

From the top
'Retro'-styled machines from Ducati's Sport Classic range contrast with the state-of-the-art 999 race replica to demonstrate the breadth of Terblanche's skill as a designer.

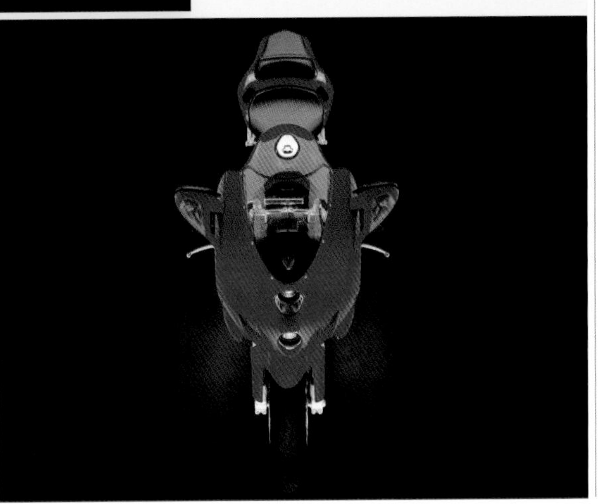

JOHN MOCKETT

Freelance motorcycle designer

Rutlish Grammar School, in Wimbledon, south London, is probably best known as the place where the former British Prime Minister John Major spent his formative years; but motorcycle fans might be more interested to learn that sitting alongside him in class was another John, John Mockett, the designer of Triumph's outrageous Rocket III.

Mockett, who was born in 1943, studied printmaking at his local art school in Kingston but a love of motorcycle racing found him spending the summer of 1964 working as a mechanic for the South African Grand Prix rider Ian Burn, who enjoyed considerable success riding Manx Norton and AJS 7R machines.

After what he considered an idyllic few months travelling around the race circuits, Mockett returned to the craft he had trained for, taking up a post teaching printmaking at St Martin's School of Art in London. Apart from riding to work on an eclectic range of machines, among them a Lambretta scooter (on which he travelled to Belgrade and back) and a 1000-cc Norvin café racer (Norton frame and Vincent engine), he was content to let motorcycles take a back seat in his life as he concentrated on his teaching career.

In the late 1960s, however, Mockett struck up a friendship with an American student of journalism who shared his passion for two wheels and spent his weekends racing a Honda CR 93 with a club. Of this period he says: "We had a lot in common and got on well, so I ended up going along with him to the races and helping him to maintain the bike.

"This got me back into the racing scene and I was also photographing the action and doing various drawings and sketches. As it turned out, this friend went back to California, where he became editor of a publication called *Motor Cycle Weekly* and he asked me to be his illustrator."

From there, Mockett began to build up his range of motorcycle illustration and photography work to the extent that it became his main source of income and he was able to give up teaching. A turning point came when he began creating a cartoon strip for Britain's weekly *Motor Cycle News* called Sprocket, which followed the adventures of a hapless biker and his friends.

"Being involved with the motorcycle press then led me to write and illustrate a piece for *Bike* magazine about the Bol d'Or twenty-four-hour race in France. The piece was all about the aerodynamics of racing motorcycles because, back then, road bikes didn't have fairing that was designed to make them more streamlined. My point was that this was the future of motorcycle design and the article attracted attention from Yamaha, who approached me to style an entirely new type of motorcycle fairing."

Although the six-month project was intended to be nothing more than a design concept exercise, the result so impressed Yamaha that the giant Japanese firm decided to put it into production on a version of its then flagship machine, the XS1100 shaft-drive tourer.

Known as the Martini 1.1 because of its distinctive white paintwork and Martini-striped livery (the aperitif

"One of the Yamaha test riders was particularly impressed with it [the fairing] because he found he could ride along the Italian autostrada wearing an open-face helmet and smoke a cigarette without having to worry about the wind blowing it out"
John Mockett

producer was a major race sponsor), the bike was one of the most imposing on the road, thanks to Mockett's unique fairing, which featured twin side-mounted running lights and a separate top section that turned with the handlebars.

"One of the Yamaha test riders was particularly impressed with it because he found he could ride along the Italian autostrada wearing an open-face helmet and smoke a cigarette without having to worry about the wind blowing it out," he says.

The impact of the 1.1 led Yamaha to employ Mockett for the next four years to help design its accessories and concept machines, which included the original Yamaha Paris–Dakar 'rally raid' race bike and a large-engined scooter with oversized wheels – effectively the late-1970s version of what was to become popular as the 'maxi scooter' twenty years later.

As part of his responsibilities as accessory designer, Mockett was once flown to Amsterdam just to arrange the badges on Giacomo Agostini's leathers before he took to the track for Yamaha in a major race.

"That actually represented an interesting step in the history of motorcycle marketing because I suggested we put the Yamaha name on the collar of Agostini's racing leathers, something which had never been done before but which is quite usual now," says Mockett.

This was around the time that Yamaha works rider Kenny Roberts decided to establish his own racing team, sponsored by the Lucky Strike cigarette company. Mockett was called in to work on the livery of the bikes as well as the aerodynamics of the fairings and stayed with the team for some time.

"One of the bikes I very much enjoyed working on back then was a Yamaha TZ250 racer which was being campaigned by the American rider John Kocinski.

"It was during the 1988 season and we tested it in Yugoslavia before racing at Imola in Italy and at the Nürburgring in Germany, where it looked as though Kocinski was going to win the Grand Prix – until he crashed when he was in third place.

"Of course he blamed me for the disaster, saying I had made the seat area too large. I was so upset I burst into tears! But aerodynamically the design was excellent, with a blunt-fronted fairing which contained internal ducting to enable us to use a small radiator.

"I later learned that the overall shape was used on a 500-cc GP machine and, when it was tested by the Japanese in a wind tunnel, it was proved to add 8 km/h (5 mph) to the bike's top speed."

His next project was with the maverick and aristocratic motorcycle producer Lord Alexander Hesketh, who established his eponymous bike manufacturing company in 1982 in the grounds of his family seat at Easton Neston in Northamptonshire.

At around the same time Mockett was approached by Heron Suzuki GB, who believed that there was a market for a small-engined car that could legally be driven solo by holders of a UK provisional driving licence.

"The concept was called the Suzuki Tripod, which was a three-wheeler with 50-cc engine. It was based on a

Left
Mockett's fairing design for Yamaha's XS1100 tourer of the late 1970s was a revolutionary, two-part unit, the top of which moved with the handlebars.

Above
Examples carrying this livery were known as 'Martini 1.1' models.

type of vehicle that was popular in France, a four-wheeled car with a 340-cc diesel engine that could be driven by youngsters. Suzuki approached the British government to introduce similar regulations to those used by the French but it didn't happen and so the project was shelved."

After that he worked for Steve Harris, the well-known producer of after-market frame kits and performance parts, whose firm Harris Performance produced the legendary Harris Magnum street bikes. Then, in the late 1980s, came the approach from Triumph.

"I was one of six people invited to take part in a design competition – I actually came second but ended up working for Triumph anyway, initially making practical modifications to other people's work. It was originally going to be a two-week project but instead of being there fourteen days I was there fourteen years!" Mockett says.

During his time with Triumph he worked on numerous concept designs and created many of the original drawings for what became iconic Hinckley Triumphs such as the Tiger, the T595 Daytona, the Bonneville, the Thunderbird and the Trident.

"My original styling for the T595 back in the early 1990s was far more radical, with an underseat exhaust and so on. It was toned down for production but it is still regarded as a significant design."

Mockett's swansong at Triumph, which he left at the end of 2004, was the Rocket III, which reveals more than a hint of his work as a cartoonist. He made the Rocket III distinctive from all angles, particularly the front, which is distinguished by its twin-headlamp arrangement, similar to that of Triumph's Speed Triple street bike – a look that has now become synonymous with the marque.

"There were all sorts of ideas for the engine – the original scheme would have had the clutch and gearbox behind, as is often the case with cars – but turning the engine sideways suited the cruiser style and the relaxed riding position. It was originally only to be a 1500-cc unit, but then it just became as big as the tooling at the factory could cope with."

Mockett's first design concept, code-named Series S1, yielded a more futuristic look, with the machine clothed in dramatic bodywork and sporting a highly stylized chrome tailpiece, but this was dropped after consumers invited to see the prototype at 'styling clinics' in the US responded badly to some of the bike's features.

Most people agree, however, that the finished product is still pretty radical.

Left
A Yamaha TZ250 racer with Mockett-designed fairing.

Above
Mockett's motorcycle design work has extended beyond machines to include race clothing. This is an idea for Barry Sheene's leathers when he was riding for Heron Suzuki during the early 1980s.

Opposite
Mockett's ideas have been used across the Triumph range. He worked on machines as diverse as the Daytona sports bike (top left), the adventure sports Tiger (top right) and the Rocket III cruiser.

ROCKET III

ROCKET III

MOTORCYCLE TYPES

TOURERS

Thirty years ago the hardened long-distance rider had little choice of motorcycle. BMW's shaft-drive, flat-twins had carved out a niche as definitive touring machines and Honda was starting to offer competition with its luxurious, water-cooled Gold Wing. These apart, it was a matter of throwing a set of panniers over your faithful all-rounder and heading for the hills.

Today it is a very different story, with every serious manufacturer offering superbly equipped, large-engined, purpose-built touring bikes that are as well appointed as some family cars.

Aerodynamically efficient fairings protect rider and pillion from the elements at three-figure cruising speeds, ergonomically designed seats ensure day-long comfort, and intercom-linked sound systems relieve motorway monotony. Handlebar grips (and seats) are invariably heated, fuel tanks can offer a range of more than 402 km (250 miles), and modular luggage systems that lock on to purpose-built carrying racks provide capacious, stylish, secure storage.

SPORTS BIKES

The ability of motorcycle manufacturers to transfer one year's racetrack experience to the next year's model range is extraordinary. Two-wheeled race technology reaches the road far more quickly than comparable advances in the car world, so much so that most road-going machines have the brakes, power and handling to make them competitive racers straight from the crate.

Huge leaps in engineering mean that 600-cc engines are now producing more power than the one-litre units of the 1980s, and extensive use of aluminium, magnesium, titanium and carbon fibre results in chassis that are light and rigid.

Combined with twenty-first-century suspension, tyre and braking technology, this makes for superb handling machines that are blindingly fast. At the same time clever electronic mapping of fuel and ignition systems ensures that a motorcycle capable of 290 km/h (180 mph) can still be relied upon to behave itself in city traffic.

As for comfort, you can forget it. Sports bikes are uncompromising, racetrack refugees that demand a jockey crouch from the rider and come into their own on a ribbon of twisting blacktop where pillion passengers just don't belong.

SPORTS TOURERS

What we call a 'sports tourer' nowadays would, not so long ago, have been regarded as a hyper-sports race replica. The power and handling of these machines leaves old-school sports bikes for dead, yet they also manage to be surprisingly practical.

With less radical riding positions than their more uncompromising pure sports cousins, sports tourers accommodate rider and pillion in relative comfort over long distances. A wealth of luggage has been designed to fit around their curvaceous flanks and tanks, yet the sleek appearance of the average sports bike won't leave would-be racers feeling embarrassed that they don't ride the real thing.

In fact, for those willing to admit that all-out sports bikes are too uncomfortable and needlessly fast for daily use, sports tourers such as Honda's VFR 800 and Triumph's Sprint ST have come to be regarded as true all-rounders.

STREET, NAKED AND MUSCLE

Street bikes are not usually glamorous or especially sporty and not always cutting-edge. These are machines based on tried-and-tested engineering and the simple principle of motorcycle as workhorse.

Those who prefer to make a statement, however, are more likely to go for the bolder, brasher 'nakeds', which are becoming increasingly popular. This style of machine emerged during the 1980s when riders began to convert sports bikes by ripping off the fairings and junking dropped handlebars in favour of upright ones to create mean-looking 'streetfighter'-style custom bikes.

Modern production nakeds are usually derived from pure sports models with upright riding positions, yet their engines are only mildly detuned and, with their state-of-the-art sports suspension, they handle equally well. Aggressive underseat exhausts and fat tyres are currently *de rigueur* on nakeds.

'Muscle' bikes are less radical and more traditional. They are physically big, with high-capacity engines, and models such as Honda's CB 1300 have a loyal following of riders who like a motorcycle to look like a motorcycle and who appreciate the bullet-proof engines and comfortable riding positions that muscle bikes offer.

ADVENTURE SPORTS

When manufacturers such as BMW, Yamaha and Honda introduced their first big four-stroke trail machines in the early 1980s, riders discovered a whole new world of motorcycling.

They found that these large, comfortable machines were ideal for exploring difficult-to-reach parts of the world. Their off-road credentials meant they could ford rivers and cross deserts, their lazy engines provided an adequate cruising speed, and their imposing size gave them the luggage-carrying ability of a small camel.

Spring-loaded gear and brake levers, flexible indicator stems and lightweight, plastic mudguards protected them from the knocks and bumps of unmetalled roads, and large-capacity fuel tanks lessened the problem of the lack of filling stations in remote areas.

These motorcycles heralded today's adventure sports machines, more of which are now sold than any other category of motorcycle. The latest have powerful, twin-cylinder engines, bikini fairings blended into their fuel tanks and unfeasibly sharp handling. With numerous after-market accessories available to enhance their considerable capability for adventure, they have truly made the world a smaller place.

CRUISERS

Harley–Davidson started it all with its large-capacity, laid-back, v-twin groundshakers that remain the stuff of dreams and legend. The company is the world's most successful producer of cruiser bikes, but competition continues to hot up in a category of machine that many riders believe epitomizes the freedom of motorcycling.

A cruiser doesn't need to be fast; it just needs to have presence. The v-twin engine has emerged as the classic powerplant, and the larger the capacity the better. Make the frame long and low, make the handlebars wide and high, and put the footrests well forward. Pad the saddle, add lashings of chrome, a fat back tyre and exhausts as mean-sounding as the law will allow. Then you've got a cruiser.

Buyers are often 'born-again' bikers with cash to spend who like the low seat height and loping gait that cruisers offer. The latest bikes handle surprisingly well too, and with a range of models from every maker it no longer has to be a Harley – although for cruiser purists, it does really.

SUPERMOTOS

Whoever thought of combining a motocross track with short stretches of metalled race circuit created an entirely new category of motorcycle that has taken the two-wheeled world by storm.

Supermotos are what you get when you put a set of wide wheels with sticky road tyres on to an off-road motorcycle.The latest models shamelessly bring out the hooligan in every rider. Firm, long-travel suspension, wasp-slim dimensions, monster disc brakes and, most importantly, a big-bore, four-stroke, single-cylinder engine put the fun back into motorcycling.

Many buyers are converted former sports-bike riders who find a supermoto can fulfil their need for thrills with its lightning handling, punchy, wheelie-prone engine and the type of stopping power that will easily stand the machine on its nose. Most have a top speed of around 129 km/h (80 mph), which makes it harder for over-eager riders to lose their licences, and as well as making great commuter machines they also offer an inexpensive way into competition – supermoto racing offers thrill-a-minute fun on tight, twisty kart tracks.

RETRO

There are plenty of older motorcyclists who regard some of the British and Italian machines of the 1970s through rose-tinted goggles; but the fact is, while they looked like rolling works of art, many were less than reliable.

Motorcycle technology has come on by leaps and bounds since then. The electrics are better, engines are more powerful, more efficient and more reliable, and the materials and methods used in frame building make modern chassis that are lighter, stronger and more rigid.

Imagine if those great-looking old bikes had been this good. Well, it seems, they can be now. Firms such as Triumph and Ducati have produced modern-day takes on the 1970s classics and managed to bring the style we love right up to date in a modern package. Royal Enfield is back, too, as is one of the greatest British bike names of all, Norton. Admittedly, it is now owned by an American company, but many people think its twenty-first-century take on the Commando beats the original hands down.

MAXI SCOOTERS

Three-figure maximum speeds, single-figure 0–97 km/h (0–60 mph) times, and relaxed long-distance cruising ability were, at one time, never associated with scooters because they had small engines and tiny wheels and worked best in strictly urban environments.

The emergence of the first maxi scooters in the late 1990s changed all that. They took the automatic, twist-and-go ease of scooter riding to a new level with their half-litre engines, aerodynamic fairings and bigger wheels. Maxi scooters can carry two in comfort and mix it in the motorway fast lane with confidence; they're even good for touring.

Practicality, however, is the crux of the maxi scooter. They offer a useful amount of storage space, their protective bodywork means you need not turn up at the office looking dishevelled, and the most sophisticated models boast features such as heated handlebars, stereo systems, electrically adjustable screens and mobile-telephone chargers.

ODDBALLS

As components become cheaper and easier to produce, consumers demand new forms of entertainment, and as conventions become ever more irrelevant, motorcycle designers become all the more imaginative.

So it's no surprise that a new, unclassifiable form of powered two-wheeler is emerging that has been strongly influenced by skateboard and BMX culture. These bikes take knocks and bumps in their stride, ooze street cred and, in some cases, can be used to perform far-out stunts.

In the Oddball category in this book you will find everything from an electric scooter to a stunt bike so pared down it is almost more bicycle than motorbike. And this is probably just the tip of the oddball iceberg.

GLOSSARY

Italics indicate a cross-reference.

AIRBOX
A chamber attached to a *carburettor* or fuel-injection system through which air is supplied to enable vaporization of fuel to take place. An airbox also acts as a housing for the *air filter*.

AIR COOLING
Air-cooled engines rely on the passage of air to dissipate heat from around the engine and usually are heavily finned for this purpose.

AIR FILTER
A foam or corrugated-card device that prevents airborne foreign matter, such as dust and water, from entering the fuel-delivery system.

ANTI-LOCK BRAKING SYSTEM (ABS)
A system to prevent loss of control caused by a wheel locking on slippery surfaces or under extreme braking. ABS electronically releases and restores braking pressure at intervals of fractions of a second to prevent wheel locking.

BASH PLATE
Protective metal guard often used on off-road or dual-purpose machines to prevent damage to the underside of the motorcycle engine from stones and other debris.

BELT DRIVE
A clean and quiet method of transferring power from the gearbox to the driven wheel via a flexible toothed belt as opposed to a chain or driveshaft. Particularly favoured by Harley-Davidson.

BHP (BRAKE HORSEPOWER)
The imperial, and most widely accepted, unit of measurement of the power developed by an engine. The corresponding metric unit is the kilowatt (kW) (1 bhp = 0.7457 kW).

BORE
The diameter of an individual *cylinder* in an engine, inside which the piston travels.

CALIPER
The part of a disc brake that presses brake pads on to the brake disc to slow the wheel.

CAMSHAFT
The part of an engine that controls the opening and closing of the inlet and exhaust valves that draw in vaporized fuel and expel spent gases. Many motorcycles have *double overhead camshafts* (DOHC).

CAPACITY
A measure of engine size, referred to as 'cc' (cubic centimetres). A 1-litre engine is described as '1000 cc'. In America engine capacity is measured in cubic inches (1 cubic inch = 16.4 cc).

CARBON FIBRE
A very light and strong material made of woven and bonded carbon that is often used to produce ancillary parts for high-performance motorcycles.

CARBURETTOR
A device that mixes fuel and air in the correct quantities and feeds it into an engine to enable internal combustion.

CASSETTE GEARBOX
A modular gear cluster that can quickly be removed from a motorcycle engine and replaced with an alternative set of gears to give different ratios. Most useful on race machines.

CAST-ALLOY WHEEL
A popular type of motorcycle wheel that is light, strong, and easy to clean and can be produced in many styles.

CLUTCH
A component that converts the power of an engine into drive to the transmission. The 'slipper' clutch, currently popular on sports bikes; eliminates the danger of the rear wheel locking during downward gear changes at high engine revs.

COMPRESSION RATIO
The ratio of maximum *cylinder* to combustion chamber volume when the piston is at the top of its stroke compared with when it is at the bottom of its stroke.

CONNECTING ROD
A strong, metal rod that joins the piston to the *crankshaft*.

CRANKCASE
A casing containing the *crankshaft* and gearbox.

CRANKSHAFT
A rotating shaft to which the *connecting rod*(s) is attached.

CYLINDER
A cylindrical chamber in which a piston travels.

CYLINDER HEAD
The 'head' of an engine, containing inlet and exhaust valves and, in an overhead-camshaft engine, the *camshaft*.

DESMODROMIC
A system of *valve* control used by Ducati in which a cam, not a spring, opens and closes the engine's valves.

DISC BRAKE
A brake that operates by pressing pads of friction material on to a disc attached to the wheel.

DOUBLE OVERHEAD CAMSHAFT
(DOHC) usually found in high performance engines. Two *camshafts* enable the inlet and exhaust valves to be closed and opened more efficiently.

DRUM BRAKE
A brake that operates pressing 'shoes' of friction material on to a cylindrical wall inside a wheel *hub*.

DRY SUMP
A lubrication system that stores oil in a separate tank, rather than in a sump at the bottom of the engine. Common in racing motorcycles, it prevents a surge of oil during hard braking, accelerating, and cornering.

DRY WEIGHT
The weight of a motorcycle without fuel, oil, or coolant.

DYNAMOMETER
A machine used to measure engine *torque*, enabling *brake horsepower* to be calculated.

ELECTRONIC FUEL INJECTION (EFI)
A more efficient but more complicated method of supplying vaporized fuel to the combustion chamber than a *carburettor*.

ENDURO
A type of off-road competition in which riders follow an unseen course in a specified time.

ENGINE BRAKING
The braking effect of an engine when the *throttle* is closed; this is particularly strong on large-capacity, v-twin engines.

FENDER
American term for a mudguard.

FLAT-TWIN
An engine configuration in which the two *cylinders* are horizontally opposed to each other. Also known a as 'boxer' configuration.

FOUR-STROKE
An engine that requires four piston strokes per power stroke.

GP
Acronym for Grand Prix.

HORIZONTALLY OPPOSED
An engine configuration in which the *cylinders* are opposed at 180 degrees to one another.

HUB
The centre of a wheel.

INJECTOR
A pressurized nozzle through which a fuel-injection system feeds vaporized fuel into the combustion chamber.

INVERTED FORKS
Front suspension system in which the *sliders* (the thick sections of the forks) are at the top rather than at the bottom. Inverted forks are currently considered state-of-the-art and are found mainly on high-performance motorcycles, although Suzuki has recently used them on one of its cruiser bikes.

KICK-STARTER
An integral, foot-operated crank used to start a motorcycle's engine.

LEADING LINK
A type of front suspension in which the wheel spindle is mounted ahead of a pivoted link.

LIQUID COOLING
A method of maintaining an even engine temperature by passing water around the engine through a water jacket linked to a radiator cooled by the flow of air. Also known as *water cooling.*

LONG-STROKE
A term used to describe an engine in which the stroke (the vertical travel of the piston) exceeds the bore of the *cylinder*.

L-TWIN
An engine configuration in which the *cylinders* are arranged in an 'l' shape, i.e. at, or almost at, a right angle to each other. A typical example is the Ducati twin-cylinder engine, in which the angle between the cylinders is too great for the configuration to be described as 'v'.

MARQUE
An alternative word for 'make', e.g. BMW and Triumph.

OIL COOLING
A method of cooling an engine whereby lubricating oil passes through a radiator. It is used as an additional means of cooling both air- and liquid-cooled engines.

OVERBORED
When an engine *capacity* is increased beyond its original size an engine is said to be 'overbored'.

OVER-SQUARE
A term used to describe an engine in which the *bore* is greater than the stroke, a feature of most modern, high-revving, multi-cylinder engines.

PANNIER
Rear-mounted luggage item that is made either of a hard material, such as glass fibre, or of a soft, water-resistant material.

PEAKY
An engine which has a narrow power band at high revs, and which makes little power at lower revs, is often described as 'peaky'.

POWER BAND
The point in the rev range at which an engine makes its maximum potential power. This is usually somewhat lower than the maximum safe rev limit.

RADIAL BRAKE CALIPER
A brake caliper that is fitted by means of bolts running from back to front rather than from one side to the other to produce a more equal spread of pressure on the brake pads.

REV COUNTER
An instrument that measures the revolutions of an engine, usually in thousands per minute. Also known as a tachometer.

ROADABLE
A word used to describe the abilities of a dual-purpose machine on tarmac. A well-designed adventure sports bike, for example, will be capable of crossing a mountain pass but will also perform well on a motorway, meaning it is still 'roadable'.

RPM
Revolutions per minute.

SHOCK ABSORBER
A term commonly used to describe a rear suspension unit or units.

SILENCER
A component of an exhaust system that muffles engine noise.

SLIDER
The moving part of a motorcycle fork.

SPARK PLUG
A component used to carry a spark across two electrodes inside an engine's combustion chamber to cause ignition. Twin-plug engines are currently popular for their greater efficiency and lower emissions.

SPEEDOMETER
An instrument used to measure speed of travel.

SPOKED WHEEL
The traditional type of motorcycle wheel, laced with a network of thin wire spokes. Particularly popular on off-road machines because individual spokes break on impact with hard objects and so provide a degree of shock absorption that protects the rim from deformation. A *cast-alloy wheel* may fracture in this situation.

STAINLESS STEEL
Steel treated to resist corrosion.

STEERING DAMPER
A telescopic friction device used to counter steering shake at high speed.

SUBFRAME
A separate, detachable part of a chassis at the rear of the main frame.

SUMP
An oil reservoir sited underneath or inside a *crankcase*.

SWING ARM
A chassis component that holds the rear wheel and pivots vertically to enable the operation of the suspension system.

THROTTLE
Term used to describe the handlebar control that regulates fuel flow to the engine, although more accurately it refers to the variable restriction in a *carburettor* or fuel-injection system.

TORQUE
A measure of the force applied to produce rotational movement, measured in foot-pounds (ft lb) or Newton metres (Nm). The majority of the torque figures cited in this book are given in Newton metres (1.356 Nm = 1 ft lb). Engines that produce high torque figures at low revs have the best pulling power for hill climbing and can accelerate more smoothly from lower revs in a high gear than less 'torquey' engines. Single- and twin-cylinder engines tend to be 'torquey', whereas multi-*cylinder* engines tend to be 'revvy'.

TRANSMISSION
A system of gears by which engine power is transformed into drive.

UNSPRUNG WEIGHT
The part of an engine that lies beneath – ie. on the roadside – of the suspension, such as parts of the wheels, the brakes and a portion of the suspension itself.

V-FOUR
V-four engines are usually arranged as two banks of cylinders, in 'v' formation, placed side-by-side across the motorcycle frame.

V-TWIN
An engine configuration in which twin *cylinders* form a 'v' shape. A typical example is Harley-Davidson engines.

VALVE
A part of an engine that allows fuel to enter the combustion chamber and waste gases to exit it. Sophisticated, higher-revving engines have several valves in each *cylinder* (five in some Yamaha engines). A four-cylinder engine with four valves per cylinder is referred to as a sixteen-valve engine.

WATER COOLING
A method of maintaining an even engine temperature by passing water around the engine through a water jacket linked to a radiator that is cooled by the flow of air. Also known as *liquid cooling*.

MOTORCYCLE SHOWS

SEPTEMBER 1 – 4, 2005
Eurobike, Friedrichshafen, Germany

SEPTEMBER 15–18, 2005
IFMA, Cologne, Germany

SEPTEMBER 30 – OCTOBER 9, 2005
Salon International de la Moto, Paris, France

OCTOBER 22 – NOVEMBER 6, 2005
Tokyo Motor Show, Nippon Convention Centre, Tokyo, Japan

OCTOBER 27 – NOVEMBER 6, 2005
International Motorcycle and Scooter Show, National Exhibition Centre (NEC), Birmingham, UK

NOVEMBER 15–20, 2005
EICMA Moto, Milan, Italy

DECEMBER 3–11, 2005
Bologna Motor Show, Bologna, Italy

JANUARY 28 – FEBRUARY 5, 2006
MCN London Motorcycle Show, Alexandra Palace, London, UK

JANUARY 2006
National Motorcycle Show, G-Mec Centre, Manchester, UK

JANUARY 5–6, 2006
North American International Supershow, International Centre, Toronto, Canada

APRIL 2006
South West Bike Show, Somerset, UK

APRIL 2006
Toronto Spring Motorcycle Show, International Centre, Toronto, Canada

APRIL 2006
China International Motorcycle Trade Exhibition, Chongqing, China

MAY 2006
New York Motorcycle Show, Rockefeller Center, New York, USA

MAY 2006
Big Bike Show, Stoneleigh Park Exhibition Centre, Coventry, UK

JULY 2006
Los Angeles Calendar Motorcycle Show, Los Angeles, California, USA

JULY 2006
ISPO Summer, Munich, Germany

AUGUST 2006
South West Motorcycle Show, Exeter, UK

OCTOBER 11–15, 2006
Intermot, Cologne, Germany

NOVEMBER 2–12, 2006
International Motorcycle and Scooter Show, National Exhibition Centre (NEC), Birmingham, UK

ACKNOWLEDGEMENTS

Many thanks to Hugh Merrell for enabling me to produce a book on motorcycles, which have been a part of my life for as long as I can remember. Thank you, too, to my friend and journalistic colleague Giles Chapman for recommending me as author, and to all the kind and helpful people in the press and marketing departments of the various manufacturers, both large and small. Particular thanks are due to Andy Dukes and Lauren Haslehurst at BMW; Andrea Friggi at Triumph; Luke Plummer and Ludovica Benedetti at Ducati; Andy Parr at Suzuki, Alan Dowds at *Superbike Magazine*; the book's designer, David Hawkins; copy-editor Richard Dawes – and, most importantly, the wonderfully patient and well-organized Helen Miles at Merrell Publishers who kept wheels turning smoothly throughout the project.

PICTURE CREDITS

The illustrations in this book have been reproduced with the kind permission of the following manufacturers:

Aprilia SpA
Benelli
Beta
Bimota SpA
BMW
Borile
Buell Motorcycles
Confederate Motor Company
Dreamcraft Studios
Ducati Motor Holding SpA
Gilera, Piaggio & C. SpA
Harley-Davidson Motor Company
Honda Motor Co.
Husqvarna Motorcycles
Kawasaki Motors
KTM-Sportsmotorcycle AG
Malaguti SpA
Moto Guzzi
Moto Morini
MV Agusta
MZ
Nacional Motor, S.A.U. (Derbi)
Norton Motorcycles
Royal Enfield
Sachs Fahrzeug- und Motorentechnik GmbH
Suzuki Motor Corporation
Triumph Motorcycles Ltd
Victory Motorcycles
Yamaha Motor Corporation